I Did It
My Way
and...
IT WORKED!

Redefining
the Art of
Entrepreneurship

Colleen J. Payne-Nabors

I Did It My Way and It Worked!
Redefining the Art of Entrepreneurship
ISBN: 0-88144-309-3
Copyright © 2008 by
Colleen J. Payne-Nabors

Published by
YORKSHIRE PUBLISHING
A division of Victory Graphics and Media
9731 East 54th Street
Tulsa, OK 74146
www.victorygraphicsandmedia.com

Acknowledgements

First and foremost, I'd like to thank my parents. Being one of eight kids I appreciate that my parents pushed all of their children to be the best at whatever they attempted in life. So, Mom I thank you for the encouragement and support you have given me. I also send a silent thank you to Dad who is no longer with us, but would be so very proud. Additionally, I thank all of my family for their continued support.

To my Husband, Donnie Nabors, I thank you for never telling me I couldn't do it, for believing in all my dreams, for being my rock, and for giving me a strong shoulder in the lean times. I'm thankful that you give me the support of your heart, and mostly for being a life partner who is strong, caring, and loving. Thank you for loving me.

I thank my son, Isam Morris Berry, III, for giving of his mom, for supporting me in following my dreams, and for encouraging me to never waver in my pursuit of entrepreneurial success. I remember those times in which you would say, "Mommy no!" Not wanting me to go back to the office. So, Isam I thank you.

Next, I thank my staff, for all of the life lessons they have taught me along this voyage. I consider my staff friends that have traveled with me on this exciting journey. I thank you each of you for your dedication and assistance.

When I started on this journey many years ago, many believed that this could not be done, but what an incredible journey this has been. If I were to have looked into my own time capsule of the future, I don't believe that I could have seen the adventure that was possible and what an incredible adventure this has been and continues to be. I'm following my dreams through three things by which I live my life:

1. Passion

2. Persistence

3. Perseverance

AND I THANK YOU!

True Entrepreneurs: Born or Made

I wrote this book to share my story with you in hopes that it will encourage you to never give up on your dreams. Since you're taking the time to read this book, I believe you are interested in finding out what it takes to become a multi-million-dollar entrepreneur. That's what I am, and more. You see, to become successful in the business world, you've got to begin with a full and complete knowledge of who you are. I started my life with the knowledge of who I was and who I hoped to become, because I know one thing for sure—success begins with two words: I am.

I am Colleen J. Payne-Nabors.

I am a business woman.

I am a woman entrepreneur.

I am an African-American business woman.

I am Colleen J. Payne-Nabors, a woman entrepreneur who is CEO and Owner of Mobile Cardiac Imaging, dba MCI Diagnostic Center a multi-million dollar company.

These are some of the ways that I define myself, but I am much more than mere words, and so are you. You have all of the potential in the world to be successful. This book is written to give you the advice that will lead you on the pathway to success. I'll make recommendations, give advice, offer encouragement, and I'll share my story. ***The push through is up to you.***

You have a dream to own your own business, to create something unique and to make the world a better place. Like you - I had a dream. My dream was to initiate a new business that would transform health care in my community. My persistence enabled a transformation to take place from Colleen Payne, Nuclear Medicine Technologist, to Colleen Payne-Nabors, founder and owner of Mobile Cardiac Imaging and MCI Diagnostic Center. My perseverance showered me with honors that humbled me beyond belief: Black Enterprise Business Innovator of the Year, Pinnacle Award Winner from the Tulsa, Oklahoma, Mayor's Commission on the Status of Women, 2006 Tulsa Small Business Person of the Year, Owner of one of the 5000 Fastest-growing Companies according to INC 500, 2007 Small Business Person for the entire state of Oklahoma, and in 2008, one of the most influential African Americans in Tulsa.

Life as an entrepreneur is not for the weak and faint of heart. Life in the business world means knowing how to stay ahead of the game, but first, you must focus and realize that in order to be in the game you've got to know the rules. I wanted to soar above the ordinary; I've accomplished that. My purpose now is to empower you with timely and proven solutions so that you also can break the mold and achieve your goals. If it worked for me, it can work for you. Welcome to Entrepreneurship 101!

The Survival Plan

Recommendation 1:

Start with "I am" statements - list who you are and who you will become.

Recommendation 2:

E.A.T. your "P's". That's right - Eat, Absorb and Totally consume the three "P's" that will keep you spiritually, mentally and emotionally healthy on your quest to unlock the doors to entrepreneurial success. The three "P's" are Passion, Perseverance, and Persistence. The three "P's" equate to hard work and commitment. Hard work and commitment equate to success.

PASSION will teach you power,

PERSEVERANCE will keep you determined and

PERSISTENCE will help you to break down barriers.

It will take all of the three "P's" to keep you on track.

Reawakening

I'll share my life story with you, and along the way, I will place in italics important life lessons that apply to any person seeking entrepreneurial success.

Contents

CHAPTER 1:

An Entrepreneur Is Born

I was born and raised in Oklahoma City, Oklahoma, the sixth of eight children in my family. We lived in a rural area where my father was a construction worker and my mother was a housekeeper. I'm not saying that we were poor; when you're a kid and all your neighbors are living just like you, your position on the economic scale doesn't really register. What I did know was that each summer, one of the eight of us accompanied our mother to help her clean the houses of other people. And that was not my forte. My sisters didn't mind the work, but I knew even then that I didn't want to spend my life cleaning someone else's house.

My mom had actually ventured into the world of the entrepreneur by selling Tupperware®. That didn't work for me either. I didn't want to be a domestic, and I didn't want to sell door-to-door. I decided that in order for me to better myself, I couldn't do anything that I felt would lessen me as a person. I don't say that to make light of what my mother did, because my parents were able to put at least six of us through college. It just wasn't my way, however, and it wasn't what I wanted for myself. Did I know that something special was going to happen? No, I just knew that I wanted something different from what I saw around me.

Ninth Grade Watershed Experience

By the time I reached the ninth grade back in the early 80's, Hertz Rent A Car had become a major corporate presence in our area, with call centers that required typing skills. It seemed that all the girls at my school, Star Spencer High School in Spencer, Oklahoma, were taking VOE, the vocational / educational class to learn shorthand and typing. When I got to ninth grade, all my friends were in VOE, telling me how much fun it was and that it was just like a big party. Right at that point, I made a decision. I said to myself, "I will never take that class. I will never, ever take VOE." Why? Because all those girls learned to type, and then when they got out of high school, they went straight to Hertz. I thought, *I don't want to work at Hertz. And the way that I can be sure I don't end up at there is by not taking VOE, because if I don't know how to type, I can't go work at Hertz.* That was how I had figured it.

Ninth grade came and went, and I didn't take VOE. In tenth grade, all my friends were in VOE, and I still said "no." Eleventh grade, twelfth grade—I didn't take it. By the time I graduated from high school, I didn't have a choice. I had no trade skill. I had to do more for myself when I got out of high school. Back in the early 80's, the U.S. workplace had become so technical that if you didn't go to college, you needed some sort of trade skill. I didn't have anything, so what was I going to do? Sit around at my mom's house? I knew I couldn't do that. I reasoned like this: If I have no technical skill, I'm going to have to learn something else. And to learn that "something else," I had to go to college.

I faced a serious problem in deciding to go to college. The counselors at my high school hadn't chosen me as a "candidate for success." Actually, there *were* three students that our counselors "chose for success;" consequently, they put all of their efforts into those students. What is interesting is that none of those three finished college. When I arrived at the University of Oklahoma to prepare for a degree in petroleum land management, I found I wasn't prepared for college. No one had ever pushed me to study. I look at my son today and the homework he does, and I realize that I never did spend that kind of time studying when I was in school. Was I that smart? No, I don't think so. I believe that our school just didn't push us to be any better. Because they didn't, I had no idea how to study when I got to college. I had to take the remedial classes. Three of us from my high school went to O.U., and even though we were at the top of our game in high school, all of us were in the same remedial classes.

The Bottom Drops Out

During my second year at O.U. in 1983-84, I watched the oil market disintegrate. All these students had decided to major in petroleum land management, and now we were looking at degrees we couldn't use. Right then I started thinking, *All right, I've taken all these science courses. What do I do with them? Throw them away or look for some other field where I can use them?*

I would honestly love to say that right then I had a magical moment where I realized, "I should become a nuclear medicine technologist!" The truth of the matter is that O.U. offered a week-long seminar right around that time to examine careers in the health field. We explored various modalities of health care and I looked them all over, thinking that most of them would require me to work nights and weekends and to be on call twenty-four hours a day.

Nursing, radiation therapy, all of the basic fields didn't sound good to me. And then I discovered a new field called "nuclear medicine." I didn't know much about it, but I did know that it wasn't open twenty-four hours a day at the hospital! I began researching just exactly what nuclear medicine was and what a nuclear medicine technologist did. I thought, *Well, the hours are good. I won't have to work seven days a week.* Even though I was unaware of other factors involved in this work, I decided to become a nuclear medicine technologist.

I began to pursue my new career of nuclear medicine technol-ogist. At that time, the University of Oklahoma program for nuclear medicine took fourteen students one year and seven the next, having no more than twenty-one students in the program at any given time. The first year I applied, the program was only taking seven students. I went through an enormous interviewing process only to hear, "You know what? We like your resume, but you didn't get in this year." I had a math deficiency, but the program directors said that if I was able to go back, take Anatomy, Physiology, and Chemistry II, I should have no problem when I applied the next year. I said "yes" and set my feet on that path.

I waited a year, reapplied and made it into the program. I'm not completely sure, but I may have been a recipient of affirmative action that year. In 1984, the University of Oklahoma had a requirement: They needed so many African-Americans in that program and for the first time ever, they took maybe ten African-American students. I just happened to be one of those students, but I had also been diligent following the program of study that had been set out for me. At that time, probably 300 or 400 students had applied, and that year, fourteen were accepted. I had made it in.

That first year in the program was designed to weed out the students who wouldn't be worth the University's investment. We took the hardest classes possible that year. The class that eliminated the most students was Anatomy, where we worked on a human cadaver. I remember being up at that lab twenty-four hours a day studying; all of us were extremely fortunate that we had an instructor who really gave us some help. She was actually a Dean at O.U. Some day I should go back and tell her thank-you. She studied with us and worked with us because she knew that this was the first time to have six African-American students in the Allied Health Program at O.U.—the most ever accepted. She worked with us to help us pass that class. After we passed Anatomy, we were pretty much on our own.

You Have Got To Be Kidding

I stayed in the program for one year, and then the program director, Paul Yurko, decided to leave. He had allowed me into the program despite my math prerequisite deficiency, telling me that if I completed the first year successfully, I could stay in the program. Unfortunately, in his absence, my situation changed. In the second year of the program—going into my fourth year at O.U.—I was told, "You know what? You're going to have to sit out a year and complete this one math class." I responded, "You've got to be kidding me! I only have one year left, I'm on student loans, I have no position waiting for me yet, I'm working two part-time jobs and trying to complete my degree." One of the professors, Ms. Barbara Curcio, came to my rescue. She agreed that what was happening to me was terrible, and she wanted to help. She found a program that would accept me where I was, with the hours that I already had, and would allow me to graduate on time. Otherwise, the program at the University was structured in such a way that I would have had to sit out an entire year-and-a-half to take my next cycle of classes. I couldn't afford to do that; I was on financial aid, so her help was just what I needed.

We found a program at the University of Texas Medical Branch, and I left Oklahoma, the first child in our family to leave the state. I moved to Galveston, Texas, where I faced a year-and-a-half of "hard labor." I had no life outside the school; all I did was study! I finished that program and graduated in 1986. Upon graduation, I made another decision. At that time, there was a shortage of nuclear medicine technologists, and I decided that I really wasn't ready to come back to Oklahoma. I moved to Dallas and took a job at Presbyterian Hospital where I worked for four or five years. And truly, it was quite a learning experience.

My supervisor, Edris Benjamin, was the most difficult person imaginable to work for, and I need to thank her for being so hard on us. She did not allow us to just sit. If you did not have a patient, your options were either to clean the department or to read a technical manual. Consequently, I chose to read, and she made me a much better technologist because she pushed me to excel in areas where I did not want to go. In fact, she *made* me go there!

However, in my heart I just wasn't convinced that my work life had to be this difficult. I took off at Christmas, deciding to look for other employment. At that time, I had been out of college four or five years with my degree in nuclear medicine. I took a job with another company based out of Dallas called NuMed. It was a company that managed a number of hospitals in terms of providing nuclear medicine staffing and full-service departments. I worked for NuMed as a technologist; the company would negotiate contracts, buy all of the equipment and manage the departments for the hospital.

"I Can Do"

One hospital where I worked was Baylor Hospital in Grapevine, Texas. From the patient's viewpoint, I was a part of Baylor Hospital, but actually I was part of a full-service diagnostic center owned by NuMed. My work allowed me to see what it was like to run my own department, to handle the mandates and all of the inspections, including DEQ, because those responsibilities rested on me. This was where I started to get ownership of an "I can do" mentality. It was there that I learned how to be my own boss. I was still a nuclear medicine technologist, but I'm convinced that situation laid the groundwork for where I am today.

Eventually, I moved back to Oklahoma, this time to Tulsa, where I first worked at St. Francis Hospital for five to six years. At the time, I was one of the few women in nuclear medicine, and the only African-American in the field in Oklahoma. Even today, very few women and African-Americans work in nuclear medicine. My work at St. Francis introduced me to SPECT imaging, which I came to love.

When I returned to Tulsa, I was probably at the height of my game. I had come from a major metropolitan city, and we were doing testing far beyond what I found in Tulsa. I had expertise in this specialty area, SPECT imaging (single-photon emission [computerized] tomography imaging), and hospitals in Tulsa had the equipment for it, but the technologists really did not know how to utilize the technology. There was born in me a passion to find out more about this branch of my field. I began to notice that satisfaction in my accomplishments was very short-lived. When there were "no more mountains to climb," I went in search of new ones.

My drive to help people—the reason I loved my work, the reason I got up in the mornings—led me to the Heart Center of Tulsa in 1992, working for Dr. Amjad Iqbal. It was there that my business—MCI (Mobile Cardiac Imaging)—was born. Dr. Amjad Iqbal asked me to go with him to Pakistan to set up nuclear medicine clinics in areas without access to large hospitals. There was just one problem. I didn't want to go to Pakistan. But the idea of taking nuclear medicine to patients who were without it planted a seed in my mind. I began to think about a way to take all of the components found in a hospital in a mobile unit out to rural areas. In two weeks, I had an entire plan of a "unit on wheels." And now, I had another problem. I needed doctors willing to use my services, willing to try something that hadn't been done before.

I had found a nuclear medicine company out of Boulder, Colorado, that would put the equipment in the truck. After that, it would just be a matter of "making it work" financially. The key to buying that truck was a company I found in Florida—Capelco—

that said in effect, "Okay, we'll give you the money, but you need to obtain five letters of intent." Five letters of intent meant that I had to find five doctors who would sign their names, saying that they would do business with me. For that, Capelco Capital would give me the money to pay for the truck. At that time I made $40,000 a year, so raising $654,000 seemed an impossible dream. I agreed.

I found five independent doctors to sign with me: I found Dr. James Higgins, Dr. Gregory McWilliams (they are still with me), Dr. Bryan Lucenta, and Dr. Herbert Littleton out of Tahlequah, and Dr. Petrasko out of Eufaula. Dr. Higgins was the first doctor I approached, and I still run his programs today. I went to his office and his office manager was really tough. I've found that office managers protect their doctors; they don't allow people in to see them. Today, his office manager and I are close friends, but when I sent this proposal to her, she threw it aside at first. Still, her responsibility was to put it on his desk, and she did. He responded, "Well, bring this woman in. I would like to talk to her." And she did.

When I met Dr. Higgins that first time, he said, "You know, I don't know what you are trying to bring to Tulsa, but if you bring it, I will use it." He decided, sight unseen, that whatever it was I was trying to do, he would allow me to do it. Again, my business was never really supposed to be a part of the Tulsa metropolitan area. It was directed toward the rural areas.

Next, I went to Dr. Gregory McWilliams who was also an independent physician working out of St. Francis. I wasn't part of the St. Francis system; I had come from a different world. I was in the St. John's/Hillcrest area; the St. Francis doctors didn't know who I was. They didn't know what I could do, or what I had already done. Dr. McWilliams said, "You know, I have no idea what it is you are trying to do, but I like the idea of having control over my patients in my office off campus." And that is what all these doctors wanted: They wanted the control to be able to interpret and read their studies, and I was able to give that to them. Dr. Gregory McWilliams also said, "I don't know what you're doing, but if you bring it, I will use it." That was my second letter of intent.

Next, I went to Dr. Bryan Lucenta, and he said, "I, too, am an independent cardiologist and would love to have autonomy in diagnosing my patients." There was my third letter of intent.

I couldn't believe that St. Francis, St. John's and Hillcrest had all of this technology, and here was little me getting these doctors to sign up in the Tulsa area. I went to Tahlequah to see Dr. Herbert Littleton who also signed a letter of intent. Finally, a physician in Eufaula signed a letter of intent. There were my five doctors. I could get my loan for the truck. I was on my way.

Either Teach Me How or You're Fired

My first truck was manufactured in Chicago. We started production in October of 1998, and during that time I picked out carpets and colors—just like you do when you're building a house. I was still working full time when we were within about sixty days of the truck's completion. I never stopped. I was also beginning my company at the same time, writing protocols and bylaws and setting up business appointments.

About sixty days before I decided to leave the Heart Center, the doctors there got wind that I would be departing—and the reason I was going. They came to me and asked to see a picture of the truck. I showed it to them, and they told me that they had had a change of heart.

"We want to invest in your company." I thought that was wonderful because I needed a big group signed on to make this business venture work. That's what I thought.

Unfortunately, we had different ideas of how this would work. They wanted to own 80 percent of the company, and they would give me 10 or 20 percent. "Give," as in "give" me 10 or 20 percent of my own company. I thought, *If they had gotten in on the early part of this venture, that might have worked, but to come in sixty days before this business is ready to start when I've got doctors willing to do this? I don't think I need them as much as I thought I did when I had no financing.*

I said to them, "You own 80 percent and give me 10 or 20 percent of my own company? I don't think so! I have done too much work on this." I thanked them and declined their offer. Next, I went to all my family and my friends, and I said, "Hey, I've got a great idea. Why don't you invest?" I didn't know that you were supposed to ask people for $50,000 or $100,000. Compared to that, I was asking for pennies on the dollar: $2,000, $3,000, $6,000, $7,000 or 1 percent of the company. I was selling 1 percent shares for $7,000. I ended up selling approximately 21 percent of the company for a total of $90,000. The truck payment was $10,000 a month, and I had to pay the first and last month's notes. That left me with $70,000.

I had taken and passed the test to become a CDL class B driver so I could drive the truck myself. I had never driven anything larger than my red Jeep Cherokee before that! The company that manufactured my truck in Calumet City, Illinois, had assigned me a personal driver to teach me how to set the truck up and make it work. His name was Gary, and he was from Dallas. Tracey Warknock, from the Heart Center of Tulsa, had left her job because she believed in my vision. She came to be my assistant and was with me in Chicago learning all this craziness on the truck! Tracy is shy and quiet, and there she was with me, lying on the ground under trucks.

Gary had told us to wear coveralls while we were in Chicago because he had us on the ground, looking at the air brakes, the oil, the fuel lines—every aspect of that truck. We spent two or three days looking at that truck—lying underneath it. He showed us how to set the truck up; that took about an hour. The equipment had to travel a certain way; everything had to have tie-downs on it so that nothing would move or become damaged in transit. There was a lot of work to it. We spent three days in Calumet City learning how to drive that truck and learning how to unbuckle and buckle the equipment.

Before my truck came off the line, a truck was completed for Reba McEntire. As the engine started the first time, everyone in the plant cheered—I figured that this was a sort of tradition to celebrate all that hard work coming to fruition. Next, my truck—my $654,000 investment—emerged. I was excited when it fired up and everyone on the floor cheered. Little did I know that the cheering was not because a long project had been successfully completed. They cheered because it *actually started.* I found out later that too many of the vehicles manufactured there wouldn't even start upon completion. Until someone decided to have a truck built, the chassis itself—complete with the lines and the tires—lay outside in the Chicago weather and too often had been damaged.

Tracy and I had our bags in the truck ready to go—we were so excited. That truck was absolutely beautiful. I had customized everything from the wood flooring to the carpet, and I made it "female friendly." Although most trucks or semis have clutches and stick shifts, I had this one manufactured with automatic transmission. Ours fired right up, and we kept it running for about five or ten minutes while we completed the paperwork. We were so happy to finally have our truck because it had been delayed for about a month! Everyone was cheering as we drove it out the gate.

We got on the road, and all of a sudden, something was wrong. We were probably no more than twenty minutes from the shop, but our driver, Gary, decided to have us pull into a Freightliner shop right outside Chicago. The truck was throwing gas and oil out, and we had to stop and get it fixed. But Tracy and I weren't worried—we just thought it was a little problem. We figured we would get it fixed, and then drive on home.

We got back on the road and before we were even out of Illinois, cars were passing us, covered over with this black diesel oil that our truck was *still* throwing out all over the roads and other vehicles. People were honking their horns at us like crazy, and we couldn't figure out what the problem was. After all, we had left Chicago just that morning! However, we had a camera at the back of the truck and as we looked through it, we realized that the oil was coming from *our truck.*

Gary made a call to find out where the *next* Freightliner shop was. We pulled in there and they patched us up but couldn't fix the problem completely. It was too big to fix on the road. And we had another problem. Neither Tracy nor I knew how to drive that truck by ourselves. We had been with Gary for four or five days, and his job was to teach us how to drive that truck. He was supposed to teach us every single thing we had to know. In addition to driving the truck, it literally took about an hour to set this truck up. Here we were, only halfway home, and we had all these problems. All I could think about was that I had patients scheduled in three days. I had to do what I had said I would. I had to get this truck to Tulsa—and it had to work! Every twenty or thirty miles I'd say, "Gary, I've got to drive this truck. I've got patients. I've got to be in Tahlequah." No, he couldn't let me drive. There was too much traffic, it was too busy, too dangerous. I needed to relax, it wasn't any big deal. But it *was* a big deal. I didn't know how to drive the truck, and I was going to be driving it in *three days.*

Finally, I realized that this guy was going to drive all the way to Oklahoma without teaching me to drive that truck. I said, "Gary, this is what we're going to do. I'm going to make you pull over at the next station, put you out, call your boss and get you fired. Then I'm going to drive this truck to Oklahoma."

"No, Colleen, you're going to tear it up—you can't do that."

"Gary," I told him, "if I had enough money to buy a $654,000 truck, I had enough money to insure it. I'm going to Oklahoma because I've got to see patients. People are expecting this truck. I've got patients that we've already cancelled three or four times."

That was when I realized I had toughened up—and in five or ten miles, Gary pulled over and allowed me to drive that truck home to Oklahoma.

Once we arrived in Tulsa and obtained the necessary repairs that were needed on the unit, we faced a serious situation. We had made a promise to our clients, and they had patients waiting for us. My primary job at this point was to get the truck up and operational—and get this company started! Mobile Cardiac Imaging had begun. We had just picked the truck up at a repair shop, which was in itself an ordeal. Our first account, our first patients, were in Tahlequah, Oklahoma, at Tahlequah Internal Medicine. My job now consisted of being a CDL-licensed driver, nuclear medicine technologist, marketing rep—and more.

In the earliest stages of my company, I had an "Entrepreneur 101" awakening: Not only was I the CDL driver, nuclear medicine technologist and marketing director, but I was also the publicist, account executive, human resources director and billing coordinator. The titles that I wore were many and never-ending because MCI consisted of just two people at this time: Tracey Warknock and me.

We had to get this company off the ground, and Dr. Herbert Littleton was our first client. He was our first because, in addition to getting the unit working, we had to have major electrical insulation work done for each side. This took about a month to accomplish so his site was the first that we had once everything was working. He was thrilled that this new technology—this service and this truck—had come to Tahlequah, Oklahoma. Historically, he had sent all of his nuclear cardiac patients to Tulsa, over an hour away, for their procedures.

While I didn't know all that much about this truck, I knew my job as a nuclear medicine technologist very well, and Tracy knew her job as a Certified Medical Assistant and a treadmill technologist well, too. Tracy also wore many hats in those days. She helped with marketing, did the billing and worked with me in supervision. I remember days that we would start out at Dr. Littleton's between 6:00 and 7:00 A.M. and would still be there some evenings until 9:00 P.M.

Cutting My Teeth as an Entrepreneur

On one occasion, Tracy and I overheard Dr. Littleton saying, "Hey, if they want the work, I have it. We are just going to keep them here all night!" Those first several weeks at this pace were excruciating. Tracy was crying almost every day. I couldn't cry because if I did, I would have no company, and it would all be a loss. I had to stay strong because we would have evenings where we would be out until 11:00 or 12:00 P.M. operating that semi rig truck, learning how to power the truck up and then power it back down.

It was a struggle initially out on the field, and then we would have to come back to our home office to bring in more business. The early days of operating and running the company were challenging; I look back today and have no idea how I was able to accomplish all of the things that I did within months of starting the company, never having run a company on my own before. There were so many difficulties, so many interesting situations and so many life lessons that I still remember to this day. I think that is what gives me credibility in terms of being a successful entrepreneur.

One of the things I did initially was to start assembling my own professional staff. I did not have many members on board, but I started with having my own attorney. We also had marketing days where we took that truck out and exhibited it because it was such a showpiece. It is a 55-foot semi, custom-built from the ground up. The interior was immaculate—just like a mobile home. It was one of the very first professionally customized trucks in the state of Oklahoma. When we started, there was another mobile company doing another form of nuclear medicine. I wanted our company to stand out so I bought the best truck and spent the necessary money to obtain a level of professionalism in providing mobile medicine that Oklahoma hadn't seen previously.

Ten years ago, mobile medicine was just barely on the horizon. I was fortunate to have the idea to start a mobile company. Once the company began, I moved out into other areas. Within months of starting MCI, I was already looking down the road at the future as to what I could do to enhance our services. The next idea that occurred to me was "what goes hand in hand with a nuclear medicine company?" Being in the field for as long as I had, I knew that ultrasound was the logical choice because most patients who needed a myocardial perfusion scan also needed an echocardiogram. Common sense told me that if I could facilitate a mobile ultrasound company, I would be able to see the same patients for both studies and run my routes concurrently—an ingenious idea! We started MCI officially in March 1998 and by March 1999 I already had everything together in terms of starting a mobile ultrasound company.

I attribute much of my early success to having passion, perseverance and persistence. When I started Mobile Cardiac Imaging, my son was only six months old. I was going through a divorce and working a full-time job as a nuclear medicine technologist for Heart Center of Tulsa where I had started and was running and operating their nuclear medicine program. Those early days were challenging! By the time we reached the second phase in the development of this company, we were a full-service nuclear medicine and ultrasound company, going into our second year. My son was old enough to understand where he and I were going and why.

Those early times were remarkable for both my son and me because living in Tulsa, we only had each other. There was no extended family, no one but the two of us. Being a relatively new mother, I hated to leave him with sitters, to feel as if I wasn't doing everything I needed to be a successful parent. Consequently, I took him to the office frequently, and I often tell how he would cry, "Mommy, no! Mommy, no!" because he knew that it wasn't going to be any short trip. My son has turned out well, but we both know the sacrifices we made to see the company become a success.

Climb Your Mountain

I am going to share with you the insights I gained in starting my own company, what I have achieved and the accolades that have come. I was diligent to do the hard work for my company and you can benefit from the insights that have "come from the trenches," the keys to entrepreneurial success that I have learned from a vast, diversified career as an entrepreneur—these are the tools that will give you the driving force you need to climb your own mountain!

CHAPTER 2:

The Visionary and the Dreamer

A visionary is a leader who works with imagination and insight. Visionaries are the risk-takers and challenge-makers. I think that visionaries are people who can dream and see "down the road." However, I am not necessarily a visionary. I've had people see me as a visionary, but I believe that a visionary can "forecast" the future—and I don't believe that I can do that. I think that people believe my passion comes from a sense of "vision," but instead of looking far ahead, what is most important to me is that I see *today*. I don't put restrictions and pressure on myself by saying that "in a year I need to be at this particular point."

When you do that as an entrepreneur, you add incredible stress to your life. You decide that in six months you need to be at point A, then in three more months, you need to be at point B, and by the end of the year you're going all the way through the alphabet to point Z! I believe that the success that I have is due to not having any external pressures on me that make my success contingent upon getting to a certain point at a certain time.

Operating in the "Now"

I believe that I see where I am today—and just beyond. My "vision" is to look at where I am right now and then look forward just a week or two from that. I don't ever try to project a year out. I don't wind up with the weight of the world on me because I didn't make this goal or that one every single day of my life. I don't have to hit a certain target within a certain time frame according to a business plan. The "true" visionary achieves in order to get to the next location and then to the next and the next. Some people do have that ability, and I think it is remarkable. However, I don't believe that it is part of my true calling.

I see the very next thing that I am going to do, but I don't put any external pressure on myself based on a particular timeline. If I am working a project and it is completed, that's great, but I don't produce frustration for myself by trying to get to point A before I am ready to get there. Maybe it's not meant for me to be at that place right now. Instead, I am living for today. That means that if I should decide tomorrow to open a clinic, then I'll do that.

As a young entrepreneur, most people want you to have an incredibly detailed business plan of how and when you will move forward in a specific direction. That business plan might make you a visionary who projects into the future, but it also creates additional stressors in trying to achieve each goal. I haven't functioned from a business plan in close to ten years. I wrote one, but perhaps six months after I created it, people stopped asking me what my plan was. Now if a bank were to ask me for my business plan, I'm not sure that would be a business partnership I would want. I am way beyond a business plan—not because business plans are inconsequential, but because that type of vision creates pressure. What happens if you *don't* achieve a projected goal? Business plans are important because they give other people a sense of where you're going—particularly the people you deal with in financial institutions. However, the entrepreneur needs more than what is written on paper as a business plan. The entrepreneur needs to see that next step, the step from today.

Certainly, I think I have vision, but do I lead solely by it? Visionaries have many wonderful dreams. Sometimes when you talk to people wanting to go into business, they have so many dreams. They are "true" visionaries, but a problem develops when a person has so many dreams that there is not one particular dream on which he or she concentrates. The visionary process can take you way beyond and way outside of where you are; that vision can become so enormous that a good visionary leader must balance that dream with action as well as words. Balance requires dealing with the real worries associated with making the dream come to pass. It requires determination. My own "visionary leadership" is based upon the "woman's intuition" part of me that says "I can," but it also involves balancing the dream with solid action. Today I am here. Tomorrow I want to get there, but I don't project years into the future. My vision is today and tomorrow.

Project Your Vision

I think that the more that you project an idea or a vision to someone, the easier it is to bring it to pass. How do you do that? By speaking that vision. Words build your vision as you tell your friend, your neighbor and the person down the block that you want to bring this certain plan to pass. Every time you repeat what it is that you want to do, you help your vision to become a reality. It makes your vision come to life.

In addition to projecting your vision, you have to have action. You have to add the kinetic energy—the energy of motion and action—to take your vision from the dream into reality. That's one reason I stay grounded in "today." If I project out too far, I can't accomplish anything. I have to function in the now. I am very aware of where I would like to go and where I would like to end up, but at the same time I have to function in the "today and tomorrow" in order to bring to pass what I want to happen.

Visions don't always become reality. No entrepreneur has had every deal work—it just doesn't happen like that. The vision I project is where I am supposed to be next month, next week and tomorrow. I am more concerned with today; that is how I lead my company. I lead my company with the vision of today. That means that I have to complete the task before me; my psyche—my inner personality—tells me that I have to complete whatever task is before me. I am functioning *now* in this space, in this time, while capitalizing off the past successes and learning from past mistakes. Right now, I paint a picture that is positive and clear for myself. As I am doing that, I can actually see that this is the direction that I need to go. My company and I have had very few failures, even though I moved into areas where I had no previous experience.

When I started the company initially, I was doing nuclear medicine. That's my area of expertise, who I am and what I am trained to do. Now I am meeting incredible challenges that don't fall into that area. I don't run away from challenges. When you become an entrepreneur, you have to lose that sense of fear that you may fail. I don't fear losing everything I have. When I started this company I was "working staff" with a specific skill set. I won't ever lose that. True entrepreneurs believe that, if they lose, they can build it again. For that reason, I don't have that fear of going out and taking the chance. I think that some people would cringe at the idea of having $5 or $10 million worth of equipment. I don't have that fear. I have built on top of past successes, but I have also reached out in the entrepreneur world and done things for which I had no background and no previous success at all. And I've succeeded.

Invest Like a Visionary

A visionary has a different approach to investment. I have three companies that have no relationship to medicine. I didn't have any past experience with them. About three or four years ago, I decided to buy real estate. My bankers initially told me that they would give me the money to buy any building that I wanted, but I thought, *If I am going to go out and buy a building, why don't I buy a building that would house tenants?* My first banker commented that he didn't think that I could do it because it would take me away from what I was "good at doing." By this time I already had three other companies that had nothing to do with medicine, so what exactly was it that I was "good at doing"? It seemed to me that I was good at whatever I touched, whatever I used my motivation to accomplish!

The moment he made that statement I realized that the relationship I had with him was probably not the best one for me. I found other bankers and started buying real estate. Did I have a past relationship with real estate other than buying my own home? No. Did I do well with real estate? Yes. Have I bought additional real estate? Absolutely. I had enough money to buy real estate. I had my 20 percent down of a couple of million dollars and wondered how I could best capitalize on this next venture. One way was to look at the commercial market. Was the commercial market where I needed to be? Yes, it was.

Investing? Or Supporting Someone Else?

I visited a number of investment houses in Tulsa, and that was the last day that I invested any money into stocks. I went to an investment house and found that I was being underestimated. The man I first met with—a man highly recognized in the community—handed me off to a junior financial consultant. As we sat in a room waiting for the "big man" to talk to us about investing $20,000 a month, every month, I noticed that the junior consultant was getting perturbed with my questions. I asked him why we should invest and in what.

"You know what?" he said, "I think that you should invest in REITs."

"REITs," I said. "What are "REITs?"

He told me that REITs are real estate investment trusts. A group of people buy the REITs, and we would invest in the return.

"That doesn't make sense," I said. "Why would I invest in REITs when I could just as easily go out and buy houses or commercial real estate?"

"Ma'am, I don't know." He was becoming more irritated with me, so I kept pushing.

"Okay, if you want me to invest that much money, why do you want me to invest it (in a REIT, specifically)?"

Finally, he looked at me and said, "You know what? You know the reason we want you to invest in REITs? It's because we don't make any money if you go out and buy hard commercial property!"

I looked at him and looked at my husband, thinking *You know what? Thank-you!* At this point, we had been to almost every investment house trying to find "the match" because if someone is going to invest your money, you want it to be a good match for you.

"You have been the best counsel for us," I replied, "and I appreciate it." We stood up, and as we were leaving, the president of the company walked in because he had had enough time to review my file. He realized that I was walking out the door, and said, "Oh no, don't leave!"

If You Don't Live in My Neighborhood

"Thank-you. Your investment counselor did such a wonderful job." Of course, he didn't know that the young counselor was really the person who put us on the path to financial freedom. I have since been able to take my own dollar and turn it into a million because of that one comment he made. I could have paid a million dollars for that piece of investment advice. We left and decided to buy commercial real estate.

I researched and I realized that whatever piece of real estate I bought would cost over $2 million, and someone was going to make a 3 percent commission which would be equivalent to about $150,000 of my money. I already knew that I was going to buy property. My husband had some free time, so he elected to go to real estate school. He earned a real estate license for commercial real estate, and as he finished, I signed the contract on the building I wanted to buy. My husband made $150,000 for three weekends of his time.

That experience could be considered a visionary expression of the "now." I don't invest through an investment firm because I realized most of the financial people who invest your money are living *off* your money! I came up with a basic plan of action. I watch you drive up, and if you are not driving a bigger car than I am, then you don't get to invest my money for me. I want to know where you live, because if you are not living in my neighborhood or you are not living down the street from my neighborhood, then I am paying for your lifestyle. Now, I am not saying that cars and houses are important, but money can reveal what your skills are. You are not the financial counselor that you need to be because you have not learned how to take your $1,000 and turn it into a million.

I have not invested any money into stocks other than my 401 (k). I invest into my company and into myself, but in terms of paying someone else's salary for investing my money, I no longer do that. I realized that I am paying you to live. Why would I invest in you? So many people approach me about investing with them, and I tell them, "I am not the person to talk to because I have already made the determination that if you are not driving a 500 SL with a drop-top, I'll invest my money myself!"

That young man helped me. We had met with so many investment counselors. One told us that we should invest $20,000 initially, and I said, "Well, that's a lot of money to invest. Would *you* invest it?"

"I am not you," she said, "and I don't have that much money to invest, so I can't say."

"Yes, but you are the financial counselor. You should have that much money to invest because you know all of the secrets that I don't."

We didn't invest there either.

The Visionary Sets the Tone

Another component of visionary leadership is that we show the way by transmitting energy to the people around us; I know on any given day the way that I lead my company affects everyone. If I come into the office dispirited, broken, depressed or angry, the whole atmosphere of my company changes. It is a rare day that I ever come into my office depressed, and *even if I were depressed,* I don't project that to my staff because I learned many years ago that I set the atmosphere in our company. I come to work every single day. I don't have to do that; I'm the boss. I come in because I like coming to work, but I know that if I come in and am having an extremely bad day or just a hard day, that energy radiates to the people around me. It's a real learning experience to see how people function off of your energy.

People work in the atmosphere their leaders bring to the job just like a fish swims in a river. If you are positive in your direction, no matter how bad your situation seems, you can guard that negative emotion from leaking out into your office. No one else has to get that overflow. And know this: Whenever the burden of leading a business is on you, you will have some absolutely horrible days.

Walk in My Shoes for a Day!

I can't imagine having anyone in this company know that I have been depressed at times. They wouldn't know if my mom was sick. I don't allow for excuses, and when people call me and say, "This or that has happened," or "I've been in the hospital," it's unimportant to me. That is personal, and it doesn't have anything to do with business. I am never ever going to tell you my son is sick. I am never going to tell you my husband is sick—and he has had minor surgery a couple of times. No one has known that because I don't project it. When I walk through the door of my office, it's business. It doesn't matter what happened at home.

Earlier in the history of my company, on any given morning I would have answered forty e-mails or forty phone calls before I got to this office. Having done that, how could I have a good day before I walked in the door? It just wasn't possible.

Now, after ten years of running this company, rarely do I take my cell phone into the house. So many bad things happen on that cell phone. I leave it in my car from the time I get to my house at 8:00 P.M. until I get up at 5:00 or 6:00 A.M. I check my e-mail and voicemail on my way to work every day; by the time I get to the office after answering that many phone calls, dealing with angry physicians and whatever, how could I have had a good morning? I've decided that when I am at the office, I am at the office. I am not going to say that I don't have bad days because I do, but I have learned that it is in the moment. It is absolutely 100 percent in the moment. Rarely will I let a "bad day" go on for weeks because I think that is the "stuff that killers are made of"—the stress killers.

You have to put an end to the bad day. I have learned in being an owner of a company that I might have a hundred bad things happen in one day. I have to deal with these "bad things" by handling them one at a time. If I tried to handle all the things that can depress me or which are negative all at one time, I would be dead. Sometimes women project so much emotion. I told someone recently, "You are crying about the small things in your life! You need to walk a day in my shoes, you need to try to take $10 and make into $100,000—that is what people kill themselves over!"

If I have a problem, I have learned that sometimes there is nothing more that I can do. I know that on any given morning, at any given point, I have done my very best. If a problem lingers, I still know I have done my best. I don't carry negativity with me. I don't allow the problem to upset me. I don't allow it to depress me. It is done, and it is over. My favorite words are "I'm done," and when I say "I'm done," *I am done.* I have learned that the problem is just for the moment.

I have done the very best because I operate in a world where, while I am not perfect, I do function very close to what is right. My problems get five minutes, and then I am done. If we have it solved in that five minutes, great, and if not, it doesn't go with me into the next day. I am not saying that I don't have nights that I don't sleep—I have them! What I have learned is that first, I have to figure out what the problem is that has caused me not to sleep. Then the next day, I can address it, come up with an answer or a solution—*and I am done with it.*

Entrepreneur 101 Takeaway:

Allow yourself to have a vision and a dream, but be a visionary "for today." Keep your eyes focused on where you are and where the next step will lead you. Set yourself free from external expectations and pressures that come with a timeline. Be the visionary leader "of the now."

CHAPTER 3:

You Must Believe in Your Dreams

Believing is important! It is part of projecting. You have to be able to speak that dream, and you have to be able to manifest it. Anytime that you have a goal, you have to reiterate it over and over, telling as many people as you can who will either believe in your dream or be a naysayer. You need all of those people. Every time you tell someone what your dream is, what your vision is and what you want to happen, it makes you stronger. For every person who says, "Oh, you can't do that," you'll find someone who says, "Yes, you can!" Then you process that data. You have their input of yes, no, or maybe. Projecting your dream allows you to come up with your own conclusion of "Can I or can't I?"

I find I am probably more of a dreamer. Dreams are what make reality happen; dreams are what make goals come true. Dreams are the things that you can see, feel and move around inside yourself. I want to believe in the things that most people think won't come true. I want to believe in the things that life can show us and make those things happen. Dreams and fairy tales all go hand in hand. Some days, I get to live a fairy tale life, but I also have people—

my staff—around me who keep me grounded. I tell people that, although I have so many accolades and awards I have won, none of that matters when I come back into this office. What matters is that when I walk back through the door, my staff is still saying, "Hey, Colleen, can you come do an injection? Can you come see this patient?" They help me stay focused, and that allows my dreams to become reality. Am I living my best life? I don't know. I think that my best life is still happening, but I also believe part of that "best life" is being able to have the foresight to dream.

I function in two worlds: the "now" and the dream. I function as a visionary for the vision of today and the vision of tomorrow. I don't let the reality of today block out the dream for tomorrow. The two live with each other, and neither one gets to rear its head too high. They are in balance with each other. I have both the now and the dream competing for my energy and time. Am I living my best life? Not yet! It's still yet to come, that is a part of the dream.

What is the dream? It's that desire that is constantly unfolding. The dream is a work in progress. The dream is what I am supposed to do with my life, the meaningful purpose of why I am here. That dream drives me forward each day. I never use the word "successful" because the dream is still unfolding; it hasn't arrived yet.

Why You Need Those Dreams

I have found that accomplishments have a short shelf life. They don't satisfy me for very long. I wish they excited me longer, but unfortunately they do not. When I see the dream come to pass, I know I've done it. It's completed. When I climb that mountain of the dream, it's conquered, so where is the next one?

We often wish for that "one dream." It could be your dream house, that dream car or the best piece of jewelry that you can afford. That is your dream for now, but once you achieve it, the satisfaction is short-lived. The entrepreneur's attitude is, "So, what else is there? What's the next challenge, the next mountain to climb?"

The dream is that force, that goal, that is always pulling you in its direction. It's the desire that says, "I want to do this." I am not "there" in terms of the dream that reveals the meaning and purpose of my best life, but I have found I can want the best of the best and acquire it. I used to find myself pondering my achievements because the satisfaction they gave was short-lived. I no longer do that; the dream is what it is. I achieve it; then I am done and moving onto whatever that next thing is!

The dream, the desire, continues to pull. It might be something as simple as wanting to travel somewhere and then doing it. It could be as large as wanting to buy another shopping center. Whatever it is, as soon as it's done, I need to have that drive for something more. I am a deal maker, a negotiator. Although I sometimes think that I should retire at forty-five, I find that people who hardly know me ask, "Why?" I believe that my best life is yet to come, and that purpose is pulling me toward it. I haven't arrived there yet. I have done a number of amazing things, and perhaps I have accomplished a great deal, but the question remains: Where is it that I am supposed to go? Even when I am uncertain, the dream within continuously pulls me to the next level. It is the dream that makes me get out of bed and come into work every day.

None of my dreams has too many things going on within it at one time. I might have two or three components to the dream. You see, I have had people want to talk to me about starting all these companies. I always tell them, "Focus on the first thing that you need to do. What is the first company you want to start? You don't have the resources, the money, the time and the energy to do more than one right now." What is primary with you? My head is not full of nonsense in terms of having so many dreams that it becomes overwhelming. That takes you back to those stressors, and I won't have that in my life. I live for the dream of today. Whatever is for today is for me to achieve, and obtain, and conquer. Once I have achieved that first dream, then I have room to work toward the next one.

Handling the Naysayers

How do you handle the negatives when people say you can't accomplish your dreams? It is part of projecting your dream to let others give you their opinions. Once you put your dream out there for them, you have to accept both the good and the bad. To be honest, you want to hear the good, the bad and the ugly because your dream may not be such a great one. The more people to whom you project your dream, the more input you receive to help you make the decision as to whether you can or you can't! When I started this company, I heard that it wouldn't work, couldn't work. Then I had people on the other side telling me that it sounded really big, really challenging, but they thought I could probably do it. Then I had a group that I probably can count on one hand telling me that they *knew* I could do it.

You have to allow those people you have projected the dream onto to give you opinions; you must allow them to come into your space, into your energy, into your field. You have to be able to accept hearing both the pros and the cons. Some people don't like to project their dreams because they believe that someone else is going to steal their idea, run with it, do something awful with it. You have to have enough belief in what you can do, in your own ideas and your own creativity. While people are giving you negative feedback, your belief will allow you to put their feedback into the right categories.

⇨ Are they giving you negative feedback because your dream is really a bad idea?

⇨ Are they giving you negative feedback because they don't want you to succeed?

⇨ Are they giving you bad information because you are not strong enough to carry out your dream?

Categorize all of those responses. Next, look at the people who are giving you positive information. Typically, positive information comes because people believe in you. You project your belief in your dream, and they are going to give that back to you. The maybes are going to come also—and they will be the people who will probably give you your best information. They will give you both sides. Based on all of this input, you have to make a determination as to what you are going to do. I do believe that you have to project your dream in order to see it come to pass.

I project daily if I have a new idea or a new thought. I tell people, "I didn't get here with you, and more than likely, I am not leaving with you. This is my decision." However, I project because I want to know their opinions. If I value their opinions, I have to invite them into my space so I can hear what they have to say whether it is good or not. Remember, when you invite people into your space, they have the right to give you all kinds of feedback. You have the right to interpret it in the way you feel is necessary.

At the end of the day, however, you are the decision maker. It's your call. It is going to be your company and your baby, your decision, your checkbook, your loss, your bankruptcy, your fore-closures—all of those are yours at the end of the day. And so is your success.

Entrepreneur 101 Takeaway:

Have dreams for your business—they are the force that keeps you going. Project them by sharing them with others. Get their feedback and consider it. Then, decide what your response is. You will believe in your dreams that much more, and you will find them carrying you to that "next place"—the next mountain to climb. Remember, success has a short shelf life. Always be open to that next challenge to take you forward.

CHAPTER 4:

Hallmarks of the Entrepreneurial Personality

An entrepreneur is composed of many different parts, and typically, a true entrepreneur seems to be composed of several different people. There is the kind person, the passionate person, the energetic person. The entrepreneur is composed of the strong business-minded person and at the end of the day they are composed of that tough, no-back-down person. You have to have all of those components, especially if you are a woman entrepreneur. Women tend not to have that aggressive piece because we are generally caretakers, nurturing and giving. Sometimes it's difficult for women to enter the fight that the entrepreneurial world demands.

A woman needs to be cut from tough cloth because it is rare that life is good every day for an entrepreneur. That just doesn't happen. Every day people will challenge you, especially men. Women are rarely challenged by other women because we tend to see business in a different way. Men, however, sometimes say things to women in business that compromise her integrity, compromise her intelligence and compromise her as an individual. They can even take a little of your soul in the early days when you first start your company. No matter what field you are in, some man, somewhere along the line, will own a company that you need to do business with and he will try to compromise you in business.

The key for a woman is to identify those weaker traits within herself early on. Otherwise, she will find herself knocked down and having to get up kicking. If you are a woman, you will find that it takes you some time before you develop that inner you, that aggressive businessperson who can come out and stand up for herself.

I have changed over the years. Now, you do business with me the way that I want business done, and if you don't like it, there are many other options. I have had to learn that. I believe women have to function differently in this entrepreneur environment. We are quickly run over, and it's often assumed that we are not the smartest cookie in the cookie jar. It's assumed that we're not very tough, and we'll be nice rather than direct, firm and hold a line that needs to be held.

For some years after I started this company, I didn't wear trousers to work; I thought that showed weakness in me because I had to deal with so many men. I no longer have that problem because I know exactly who I am. The moment that a woman shows that she can stand toe-to-toe and can handle whatever is dished out, she gets labeled with that infamous five-letter word: B-I-T-C-H. Oddly enough, I rarely ever hear a man being labeled negatively because he is tough. He's considered stern, but a good boss, fair at the end of the day.

Women, on the other hand, often get slammed, called names, and of course, if you are an African-American woman, those names get used even more often. As an African-American woman in business, I wear those names as badges of honor. I don't have any problem with that just as long as no one calls me these names to my face. I have learned to stand toe-to-toe with people who try to challenge me. Now, if you challenge me, you best "come with it" because I am going to give you all that you expected plus some so that I win. And I always win.

That goes for my employees, too. I have employed many male engineers and service providers, and the first thing I know, they want to say that any problem is because I'm a woman. I say, "No way." I don't put up with that, and in terms of me being tough, it has nothing to do with you and me personally. The moment that you cross the door, you become an employee of mine, and you don't get to challenge my authority.

Women frequently spend their first years of entrepreneurial life having people constantly challenge them without knowing how to stand up and fight back. Then one day you realize, "Wait a moment. I'm the boss, and my employees are challenging me? Oh, no, no, no—that's not happening!" Some of the things that have happened to me in terms of my employees never would have happened to a man. For that reason, while I am a woman, I don't *function* as a woman in my company. I'll tell you right now: if I ever come to my job and cry, everyone needs to leave. That just doesn't reside in my personality in business. I realize that when women are being good entrepreneurs, they get labeled as something else; that's fine with me. Just don't say it where I can hear!

If you are a woman in business, you will have to be a little bit tougher than almost anybody around you to succeed. Many of the women-owned businesses are the first ones to fold. Much of that is because we don't know everything we should. We are not in that "good ol' boy" network, we don't have all the bankers, lawyers and accountants as our best buddies. Early on, I found that I was part of several organizations composed mainly of men, and I realized those were the ones for me. I didn't care how you built the pool, I didn't care what colors you decorated the house. That's not to say that I am not a good decorator—I am, but I would rather sit and talk with your husband because I want to know what banker he is using, who is his lawyer, who is his accountant. Where is he getting the best deals? Those are the things that I needed to know early on.

It's Time to Toughen Up

Women, if you are planning on staying in business, you need to grow that extra set of testicles. You have to be tough. I don't think that you need to lose your femininity in the process; you just have to become a businesswoman. You can be two people inside, functioning and operating as one, but you must have that tough, strong side in order to survive.

I don't get challenged much anymore because my presence exudes authority. I don't know when I developed it or what day it was that I woke up and people knew that I was in charge. I still look the same. I don't walk or talk any differently, but my presence commands respect. This is something that just develops over time. You just wake up one day, and it's evident that you're the boss. I can be in a room, and people will know without me saying a word that I am the boss.

I have been in many meetings. My business card still says Director of Operations, and my administrator is the Administrator of the company. Often, I will let her talk because I am just listening. I want to know how you talk to her, because if you don't talk to her the right way, we don't do business. It can be a hard walk for women to get to the place where they have a commanding presence when they walk into the room. I know that I have developed that.

Learn to take charge and know when to do it. I find this is especially important for Southern women. We are trained to be courteous, but we are also trained to be subservient, not to rock the boat, not to create problems, not to disagree with the men.

When I first started this company, I was subservient. I was trying to be a woman in business, but I would bring those men lunch and dinner, simply because they were doing their jobs. They weren't doing favors for me. As I look back, I realize that I thought they were doing favors for me. No, they were doing their jobs, and I was doing "my job" of catering to men. One day I realized, "No, I am in charge here. They are not doing me any favors." Once you get paid to do a job, it is no longer a favor, but that was a hard lesson to learn. This isn't doing favors; this is business. Now I say, at the end of the day it is always business and nothing personal.

Maybe you think that doesn't sound like your personality, and you decide, "I can't operate that way." You can't know whether or not you can "do" this until you start trying. You may not know what your limitations are. Sometimes women are very aggressive. Do you know when to bring that aggression out? I have learned when to do that. There is normally no reason for me to be aggressive; my presence tells you exactly what you need to know about me. If I do need to be aggressive, I do not have any problem with it. When it comes to business and the survival of my company as opposed to the alternative, I am always going to do the right thing. If you make me bring that "alter" personality out, I can do it. I have that ability, and I know it.

I think that because women function differently from men, we can be very aggressive in our business relationships without having them become adversarial (like two men having a toe-to-toe.) I can bring out that aggressive business personality when it's needed, and when I am finished with those men, I can get up and just walk away. Two men can't do that; I have watched my husband interact with business people. Sometimes he doesn't like the way I handle them, but I will end the meeting rather than let him do it. If he ends it, it will become a conflict.

Somewhere along the line, women learn to gauge when other people are taking over, and decide, "This is what I need to do. This is how I am going to do it in order for this business, this plan, this meeting, to work." Use that ability to bring aggression without conflict.

Entrepreneur 101 Takeaway:

Learn to develop and release the necessary aggression in business that will make you a confident leader who exudes authority. As a woman, you'll need to toughen up. Remember that you're in charge—and others will recognize it, too.

CHAPTER 5:

I Knew I Could Fly!

In the early years of my business, I had so many external factors influencing me in terms of whether or not I could make it in this business. From the first moment I started the company, my goal was, "Let me make it a year." The first test put before you by the bankers, the accountants, the professional people, the naysayers, the people in your world who allow you to exist and who give you credibility that you are not a fly-by-night company and that you have substance, is that if the company survived for a year, it would mean that you could "make it."

I reached my year and "they" raised the ceiling on me, saying that I had to survive for three years. I kept moving along and working, working, working until I realized that I had reached the three years. Sure enough, the issue was, "No, no, no, we have changed the rules, and now you have to be in business five years in order to be successful and know that you'll make it. I kept moving ahead, thinking that at some point, I was going to "get there." Life was going to be good, all of my hard work would be done and I could sit back, coast and just relax. I finally hit that five-year mark, and, lo and behold, "they" raised the ceiling again—and then somewhere between years five and seven, magically I had made it.

You Can Soar Free of What "They" Say

You have a business with a plan, one that is gratifying, that's moving and you are motivated to keep it going. "They" are the people in this environment that you do business with, who give you credibility. One area where you must have credibility is your credit worthiness. You would prefer that the burden of your credit worthiness would be on your business and not you personally. However, the small business entrepreneur is always personally the source of credit worthiness. Because of that, ceilings remain in place above you. That invisible ceiling is your credit worthiness, your relationships with the banks, your accountants and all of these people who tell you that your company is not going to fly.

When I reached the five-year mark, "they" said to me: "You know what? This ceiling was almost gone, but you didn't quite make it." Finally, within myself, I stopped checking to see where that ceiling was, if it was one year, three years, five years. I had hit all of the ceilings, and I was still in business, still making it. Somewhere between years five and seven, I knew that I could fly—this company could stand on its own. I could stand alone, and together we made a force to be reckoned with.

MCI could stand and so could I. I knew at that very moment that I was free to develop the company without fear of not being able to succeed, without fear of not being able to conquer those mountains. I was free to explore life despite people saying, "You know, this company is not going to make it. You are not financially strong enough." At this juncture banks gave me opportunities that they hadn't given me before. Money became easier to get. In terms of trying to get capital and assessing the company, everything became easier. Between year one and year five, everything was a struggle because 80 percent of the people believe that you are not going to make it while the other 20 percent knowledge that you can comes from you, from within.

Time to Soar

Somewhere between years five and seven, a magical door opened and at that very moment I soared. I had been putting the pressure on myself to make the company survive, and the initial books that you read about being an entrepreneur give you time-lines. In anything you do, you want a beginning and an end, and you want to know what the middle is. It's the same with small business. I started October 10, 1998—my beginning, my entrance. That is good. Now, where is the middle? Where is the end?

I believe from the day you begin a company, you have to have an entrance strategy, and you have to have an exit strategy. The day that you start your business, you need to plan for your exit, and most of us don't do that because we always believe that we are going to be in business forever. Even if I chose to run this business for twenty years, what is my projection for twenty years from now? What is my projection for five years from now? How long do I anticipate doing this? It doesn't matter if you are the CEO of Coca-Cola® or anything else, you have to begin a business with the best starting philosophy possible, but on the same day that you sign the paperwork to start your business, you need to have an exit strategy. You have to know how you are going to leave. Are you going to leave standing up? Are you going to leave upright? Or, are you going to leave lying down?

You're Soaring When You Determine How You Leave

I wish I could say that when I started this company, I had both my entrance strategy and my exit strategy set, but I did not. About four years ago, I attended and spoke at the Black Enterprise Conference in Dallas. There was an African-American woman in attendance who had just bought one of the largest chains that supplied foods to companies like Taco Bell® and Kentucky Fried Chicken®. The one thing I heard from her that impressed me most was that she had just bought this new business, and she was talking about an exit strategy. I sat there thinking, *I have no idea what an exit strategy would look like for me.* I didn't have a retirement plan in place. I didn't know when I wanted to leave this company. I had never thought about an exit strategy for me. I just knew that I was running a company that I was enjoying—and I still love it—but at some point I was going to need an exit strategy.

So, roughly four years ago, I started planning my exit strategy: I decided that age forty-five was my time to exit. Whether or not I actually leave this company, I should be financially well off enough to stay, go or do as I please. Part of my exit strategy is not necessarily to leave MCI Diagnostic Center, but to come up with a plan where I am financially free. And once you become financially free, your life is your own. You answer to no one, and that is living the American dream.

If and when I choose to leave, it's on my own terms. It is not because I'm tired, I'm old and I've done it all. It is based on the fact that I am financially free, and maybe I'm not having as much fun as I want. I think that in order to be successful in any entrepreneurial venture, your business has to be something that you're passionate about. The moment that you lose that passion, it becomes just a job—and most entrepreneurs originally chose the entrepreneurial route because they did not want to have a job. They chose to have a career and a passion for as long as it remained exciting and interesting for them.

Age forty-five is an arbitrary number, but I do want to reach that number, and actually, I'm there! I have made a number of commercial real estate investments, and I am in a place where whether or not I leave MCI, I will be comfortable and able to sustain the life I want.

This is part of flying and soaring. It's part of exploring your wings to say that I know I am free. Sometimes our world and our society in which we live have done us an injustice. I always say that the government should have seen our earning potential and given that to us while we were young while we could go explore and travel the world. Instead, we have to wait until we are older. At sixty-five, if we are lucky, the government will give us a check and we get to sit at home; most of the fun is over. I really believe that the government should have seen my earning potential, given me my money up front and then made me go to work at sixty-five. At that point, I would have done everything, and I could just take my medicine, go to the doctor and go to work every day.

Part of flying is being good enough to know that it is time to go, wise enough to know that you can soar, and strong enough to know that it is okay to exit while you are still in perfect health so you can do all of those things that are exciting and exhilarating.

Several years ago I hired a consulting company. This consultant assessed my company and now, every December, I sit and do the same thing. I have done this for ten years, and I think that is part of what has made me successful. During that time, I set no appointments, I make no heavy commitments, but I assess my company from top to bottom. When I brought in this consultant, he said to me, "You need to take about three months off because you are a workaholic." I thought to myself, *How depressing that someone would come into my business, assess me and tell me that I needed three months off because I am a workaholic.* I thought for such a long time about what I would do during those three months.

Wear It Like a Badge of Honor

When he came in two or three weeks later to give me his final assessment, the one thing I said to the consultant was, "I wear what you said about me as a badge of honor! I am a workaholic, but that is how I got here, that is how I stay and I make no bones about the fact that I work and that I enjoy working. So, what would you have me do? Stay at home? And do what?"

I consider being a "workaholic" something I wear with pride. I am a workaholic, but I enjoy what I do. I don't have any issues with that. Loving what I do is a part of loving who I am. Choosing to stay even when I'm prepared to go is part of learning to fly.

And I am flying! After ten years of doing all of the things that I could possibly want to do, I am flying. I am soaring. I have won so many accolades that I can't even imagine the ones that I might not have won! I mean, am I entitled to win any more? I mean, what else could I win? I think that the award of which I am proudest was being named 2007 Small Business Person for the entire State of Oklahoma. I'm probably the first African-American woman to ever receive that honor. What else is there? What other award could I possibly win that would be as significant as that to me? If that is not flying, then what is?

Your Passion Makes You Fly

I constantly say that I have won so many awards that I have run out of people to go with me to receive the awards. I actually have to entice people to go to these galas with me because I have worn my family out. My husband didn't even go with me to meet Bill Clinton because I have won so many awards! I know that everyone is so happy for me and I appreciate that, but I also know that their attitude is, "What now? What did you win this time?" I still love the challenge, I still love competing, but in this room, those people were enamored by the fact that I had received so many accolades. They wished they could have just half of the awards I do; I didn't recognize how significant and how important these awards are to others. I had already said that if I never received another award, I was fine with that.

I have awards that I don't even have displayed in my office. I'm glad to have them, but I don't know that business ever gets any easier just because you win awards. It doesn't matter how big you become, if you are a hands-on manager, your hands still get dirty. They rarely ever are clean because of the decisions that you have to make on a daily basis. What remains are not the awards, but the passion within me to run this company. It is because of that I am flying!

Entrepreneur 101 Takeaway:

You can soar when you know that your survival doesn't depend on others, but on yourself. Plan to start your business and plan for your exit. Create your own exit strategy for the day you are ready to move on, but until then, soar with the passion that started and sustains your business.

CHAPTER 6:

You Have to Start Before You Succeed

So many new entrepreneurs want the glamour, the glory, the recognition and the accolades that come with having your own business. The problem with that is when you get all of those accolades, if you do not have a successful company, what are the accolades worth? If at the end of the day when you go home, that business is nowhere close to being successful, if you are one step away from bankruptcy and one step away from having your best employee quit, where is the success? You have to start your business before you can wear the mantle of success. Success comes. It is earned, not given. We do not meet people in this lifetime who have been "given" their success. Even Donald Trump's children who were born into success, still have to earn their own.

To be successful you have do the hard work of starting your business. You have to run it, manage it, market it and do the HR for it. The beginning of any business is the most important thing you will ever do. I say that because I have had many people sitting in the chair across from me in the beginning stages of their business, who have already been "successful" simply because they declared they had a business. They don't have a successful business. They just have a business, and they need to work it, grow it, love it, invest passion in it. They need to lay the foundation. One of the most important parts of your endeavor is the foundation of your business. You can never ever go back. It is just like building a house. If you ruin the foundation, the foundation is always going to have problems. You will always know that the foundation you built your house on is weak.

Everything that I do, I do to protect myself and my companies. We have one of the best, solid foundations, and I know it's because it's "The House That Colleen Built." If I had ruined my foundation, I don't believe I would have been able to climb such a high mountain.

There are steps to laying a great foundation. First, if you are going to be an entrepreneur, have an area of expertise or at least some idea as to what you are going into and why. Know what it is and why you are doing it. If you are considering a business, there are going to be so many questions to answer, so many classes to take and so much that you are going to need to learn. Laying a solid foundation is going to be the most important thing that you do.

Second, get the support you need. You want to make sure that you have the best professional staff that you can afford at that time. You are not going to have many financial resources when you start out, and you will change your professional staff as your business grows. If you have no financial resources but a particular business in mind, you will want to figure out how best you can fund it. In fact, if you can fund it internally without investors, do it.

Protect Your Passion

People frequently want me to invest in a venture that is dear to them, but I have never invested in a business venture of an entrepreneur who had passion for his or her dream. At the end of the day, you will be sorry that you had someone invest in your vision. I did that, and so I speak from experience. If you can start your business without a business partner, do it. That partner will take away much of your autonomy. That is why I won't invest in your venture. I do not want to be the one who takes your passion away. People did that to me. I allowed investors into my company, and they wanted me to stop the growth of my company because they wanted the financial rewards.

Third, you need to know the basic skills of survival you will need to run your business. This goes back to your professional staff, your record keeping, the financial management, the personnel management, the marketing analysis, the break-even points, what product or services you are going to provide, your legal structure, the communication structure, taxes, even information as basic as the way the company is set up, whether it's C-corp, S-corp, L-corp, or LLC. Who are your competitors? Is this a specialty niche market? There really are very few businesses that someone hasn't already considered. How do you take what they have done and make it better? Whenever there is a business, there is always room for improvement.

If you are a woman going into business, what are the special obstacles that you will face? I went into a man's environment, and I didn't at first realize that it was one, so that was a major obstacle for me. I had a 55-foot motor coach that needed to be driven by a man because it needed basic repairs that I couldn't make. I had a very good niche, but I also had a competitive market. I was in a science technology area that is typically not woman-based. You want to know what the obstacles are for you and how to move beyond them.

Entrepreneur 101 questions to lay your foundation:

⇨ Who are your competitors?

⇨ What are the most important factors that would cause your business to fail?

⇨ What do you need to look after immediately in terms of what a particular company did or what will happen if you don't have X?

⇨ What are the pros and cons of starting this business?

⇨ What kind of market study is currently out there? You want to know where your market is. I was running a nuclear medicine department for a group of cardiologists, and I was able to see firsthand that people were traveling hundreds of miles to come into town to see our physicians. That told me immediately that the rural area was under-served, and if the rural area was underserved, that was where my market was. This just came about from observing people having to take off work and go get Mom and Dad and drive them to and from Tulsa. I had a niche market right before me. If I could serve it, there was my business.

⇨ How are you going to develop and determine where your market is? I was in medicine so I knew where my market was and I knew where the patients were. I knew what services they needed. My market research came naturally because I stayed in the environment in which I was starting my business. I knew where my market research was because I was in that industry. I knew who the physicians were, where the hospitals were and who was doing what in my industry.

⇨ How long is it going to take to build the business? This is where all the glass ceilings appear.

- Is this a one-year ceiling, a three-year ceiling or a five-year ceiling?

- How tall is that ceiling?

- Can the ceiling open up and close back?

- How long is it going to take you to get where you are going from a success standpoint?

These are all important questions, but the key factor is your banker. The most important aspect of any entrepreneur relationship is the banker. Know your banker. If you and your banker have exchanged all your personal phone and pager numbers, you have got a good banker. I'm going to discuss the importance of your banker in greater depth.

Entrepreneur 101 Takeaway:

Success is not the glamour and flash of owning your own business. Instead of trying to be successful, start first by doing the hard work of your business—the homework, the research, the labor—real success will come because you earned it.

CHAPTER 7:

Start with the Best

Starting with the best goes back to examining your market, understanding who your competitors are, and finding your niche. When you are starting a company, there are so many people who will not want you to be successful. So how do you start your business and do a really good job? You want to look like the very best of what you have to offer. If you are going to open an office to do janitorial work, you want that office to look like it is a janitorial service. If you have clients come in, you want your office to be neat, organized and orderly. You want everything sparkling clean.

What if you were to take that same company, put it an office with trash all over? When people come in, what is the first impression they will have? "If you can't maintain the cleanliness of your company, then you certainly cannot maintain mine." Appearance is everything—it's your opportunity for a first impression.

If You're in It to Win It, Don't Cut Corners

When you meet someone, apply the "Five-Minute Rule"—that means you make a quick assessment of them. It is the same thing with your business. When you start a business, if you are in it to win, you will want to play to win. That means that you want to look the best you can and be the best that you can. If you have $9.99 to spend, then you want to spend the whole amount. You don't want to cut the corners and just spend $5, because that very corner that you cut could be a public corner that you are cutting where people will notice and make assumptions about your business.

We all have to cut corners in terms of business, but you have to find the areas that are going to have the least impact in which to cut corners. That means that when you start your office, presentation is everything. You may not be successful and a lot of us are not successful when we start, but if you walked into my office, you wouldn't know that I wasn't successful on the very first day of business for any of my clinics.

When I opened my clinics, we had virtually no patients for almost four months. It was barely worth keeping the office doors open, but the "Three P's" I live my life by—Patience, Perseverance and Persistence—kept me soaring. I wasn't successful. I had another business, of course, that funded several ventures, but when you walked into my first clinic you could not tell it wasn't successful. I spent what I needed to in order to look my very best, and you would not have known that you were not at a hotel. You didn't feel as if you were in a sterile doctor's office or a cold hospital clinic. That is why presentation is everything. Those patients who came to our clinic returned and told their doctors that our center was absolutely gorgeous! Eventually, those physicians started to send more patients.

I knew that if we looked good, people felt it was more than likely that we were good. Your clients want to see that you took time, energy and money and developed that into what you are today. When you start with the very best, you leave little room for the people with whom you are competing to speak negatively about your business.

This was true in terms of medicine and diagnostic imaging. We can't always buy a $4 million scanner like the hospital. That will be the first thing your competitors notice. But at the end of the day, we have a scanner that will give the same results—it just doesn't have as many bells and whistles. We may not have the $4.2 million scanner, but we have a $2 million scanner that does the same amount of work, looks as good and gives the same report. Remember, perception is everything. Perception is reality.

Looking the Best Pushes You To Be the Best

Another reason to get the very best that you can afford is that if you spend that amount of money buying the best, you are going to think twice about not pushing your hardest every day. You are going to think twice about not doing your very best. You are going to think twice about not being conscientious about the products and services that you offer. If you have invested your time, your energy and your money, do you want to fail? No, you do not, so you tend to work harder because you have more invested. If you take your last $200,000 and use only $50,000 of it to start your company, every day you walk in, you'll think, *I should have bought one or two levels up on this piece of equipment.* I have never made that mistake in anything that I have ever done with my businesses.

When I walk into any of the centers that I own, they have the very best I could buy; it stands up and competes with all my competitors. I walk into my center today and there is not one thing that I would replace. When you have that, it gives you a level of success that you feel good about every day. However, if you walk in your business daily, and you think that instead of spending $20,000 for this, I should have spent $27,000 and bought the very best, you will constantly be fighting an internal battle with those negative reactions that will eventually cross over to the image of your business and take energy away from it.

There is not one thing that I would have done differently in our office because I did the very best I could. It makes you proud and confident. I don't think there is one thing I would replace. I was very detail-oriented in creating this office. I brought my carpet in from North Carolina. I had custom furniture made in California. I am in Oklahoma. I could have easily bought what I needed in Oklahoma, but I chose not to do that, and when I walk in every day, I am not distracted by wanting to replace everything and feeling that I should have done more. I'm not saying that you need to order *your* carpet from North Carolina. I'm saying that the moral of the story is to do the best you can because it will pay off.

Starting with the best puts a competitive edge on you; if you believe that you should have done things differently, then so will your competitors—and they do stop by. They will come to your place of business. They will see what you have. We have had so many competitors actually come to our office. As they are walking in, you know that they are looking at your work of art. You know they are going to have the same thoughts that you have, but you also know that they are going to criticize you much harder than you do when you walk in every day and think, *I should have.* They are going to say, "You didn't do it." Start with the best you can afford and if you can, maybe extend a little bit beyond the best. Doing a little more research gives you that sense of pride. That translates into a positive energy that everyone coming into your business feels.

Entrepreneur 101 Takeaway:

Start with the very best you can—make your business appear the most attractive, the most appealing, the most professional you can. Pay attention to the details from your building upkeep and furnishings all the way to your letterhead and business cards. When you spend your money on the best you can at that time, you remove the "criticizing points" of your competition—and you eliminate the negative energy of regrets by replacing it with the positive energy of excellence.

CHAPTER 8:

If You Ruin Your Foundation, You Can Never Build Higher

The foundation an entrepreneur creates is key to success because what you establish is what the world sees from that day forward—and people rarely forget. Sometimes you are able to reprieve yourself and make a bad situation good, but it is rare that you get a second opportunity in business. That's why your foundation—what you start with—has to be built on solid ground.

Part of your foundation is the physical presentation of your building. That building can be you as an entrepreneur or you as an individual or can represent your business. You want to look the very best you can. Obviously, there is the importance of first "looking good" on paper. Then, you want your facility to be attractive; that is the foundation that you are establishing. Next, many new entrepreneurs sometimes forget about "the paperwork." If your office uses faxes, forms and letterhead, do they look the best that they can? Unless those details are your forte, they may not be the best. Consider the building that you are in, its landscaping, and what you have in the building that's part of your business, the letterhead you choose, business cards, fax forms. That is the physical foundation; once it's in place, people want to examine your "core" foundation.

Your Core Values Are More Than a Plaque on the Wall

The core foundation consists of the values on which your company is based. This foundation is more than just a mission statement. Sometimes we put the mission statements on a wall, and that's it. It's just words on paper or on a plaque. How often do you really look at your mission statement? Is that mission statement still valid and ongoing for your company? The core foundation is what everything else in your business relies upon. If you build your company on strong ethical and moral values and "do right" principles, that is the real foundation that you are built on. If you start your company with indiscretions, with not being truthful or honest, with making promises that you can't deliver, you have created a foundation that will keep you from soaring to the highest level. If you ruin your foundation, you will never build your company to the heights it could have reached. That core foundation that you are building has to be intact; that is one of the most significant aspects of my business that I have protected all of these years. I have watched over my foundation because once you ruin your foundation, it becomes very difficult to rebuild the image of you and your company.

My foundation is me. It is me publicly, because while I don't have the glitz and the glamour of movie stars, people often forget that when you become any kind of public figure, you really do give up your life. Too many celebrities forget that they chose to be in the paper, they chose to be in the public eye, and now that their fans have made them, they are watching closely. How many times have we heard of movie stars who suddenly want to avoid the fans and photographers they once courted? When they chose to be a public figure, that's what they became. It is the same way in terms of business.

The Merging Into One Entity: You and Your Business

Whether or not people are watching me every day or whether they watch me once a month or once a year, I'm on public display and that public persona goes hand in hand with my business. If I ruin my company, I have ruined myself. If I ruined myself, then I have ruined Mobile. We are one and the same in the public's perception. The foundation that I stand on is a double one: I stand as a business owner, and I stand as a public entity. I have been able to maintain both of those entities without ruin. I am out saying, "Trust me, I am a good businesswoman"—and I make no bones about that. I stand toe-to-toe with my competition, and I handle all of my business every day. Because of that responsibility, I no longer allow people to challenge my authority.

This may not be the best path for women, but it has become a good business practice for me. I have made decisions which people might not respect in terms of my business acumen, but do they respect me as a businesswoman? Do I play to win?

Absolutely. Those decisions did not ruin my foundation; they are just good business.

If I were to open the book of my life, could someone say that I was just an unpleasant person? No. Am I a bad businesswoman? No. Is my foundation sturdy and strong? Yes, and I have protected that. The foundation of your business is most important for any entrepreneur to protect.

I realized about four or five years ago that I had become one and the same with my company. The company and I had so merged that I began to be concerned about what would happen to my employees and their families if something were to happen to me. I spent the next three years of my life separating myself from my company. What if something unforeseen happened to me? I told my husband a long time ago that if the worst happened, to sell this company and sell it before I was buried. Otherwise, it wouldn't be worth the paper it was printed on because this company was based on me. That was then.

Time to Separate You and the Company

Today, neither this company nor the other companies we own are based on me because over 75 percent of the business we see is no longer personal, and the customers no longer know who I am. It appears as though it is a franchise and that we are some really large group. That is just part of being able to separate your foundation from the company's foundation and allowing you to stand on your own. I think when you and your business are the same entity, that is where the problem comes in. Many companies get in trouble, and when there is just one person at the helm of that company, the stock goes down. I want it to be known that this company stands on its own and that it is not just Colleen's company. It is MCI or real estate.

If I do something extremely bad, then I am the company. If I have an unforeseen accident, there will be just a small blurb in the paper: "She was the owner, but the company continues." However, if I do something terrible, we are both ruined.

You do things that call attention to yourself and then all of a sudden you don't like the attention anymore and you don't want us to watch. We still get to watch because we made you and in some regards that is part of where I live. You know, I don't think that anybody made me, but if I do something inappropriate the wrath would be great, because it would be both me and the companies we own.

Protect Your Foundation with the Truth

In my mind I just don't see how I could ever be unethical, and I always make a disclaimer to people, "I am always honest." It really is sad to make that disclaimer, but sometimes I tend to be so truthful and I say things that could be hurtful, but it is the truth. I have tried to stop doing that because when I make that statement, "I am always truthful," what that means is that I am going to tell you the truth, and it may not be appropriate for you. You may not want to hear it, but I am going to be true to me and I am going to tell you.

Sometimes people don't like to hear the truth. They want it sugarcoated. I can do that, but even if I sugarcoat it, I believe that I have only got a couple of minutes to tell you what I need to tell you so I can make the statement, "I am always truthful." Whenever I say that, whatever comes after that is what I have thought about and I know that is probably an appropriate thing to say, but you may not take it as well because sometimes we don't like to hear the truth. I always want to hear the truth, no matter what. It doesn't matter what it is, I don't have time for you to run me around the corner. Tell me the truth. The truth protects me and protects my business.

Entrepreneur 101 Takeaway:

Your foundation is critical to your success. At the beginning of your company's life, you and the company are perceived as one and the same. Live in a way that makes you and the company truly "squeaky clean"—always operate by what is true, ethical and right. Your foundation will be strong—and will allow you to build to the heights that you want to reach!

CHAPTER 9:

Redefining Success

I rarely ever use the term "successful" in regard to myself. People may describe me as successful in terms of what they believe I have done with my life, but I think that success is where you have set your own goals, determined how to reach them and have channeled the various areas of your life toward meeting those goals. Success comes from within. It is earned, not given to you by someone else.

What is the measurement of success? Is it how well you work? How much money you have? Is it the number of accolades that you received? Success applies to the life you lead, and it can consist of any number of elements that work for you. I think that I am successful in my life, but I don't approach the idea of success the way most people do, putting false expectations on myself. Suppose I have the expectation that in five years I am supposed to be at point Z, and at the end of those five years, I am not there. Does this mean I am not successful? What if I got to X in my mind without any preconceived expectations? The way I look at it, I am successful because I got to X when I really wasn't supposed to leave A. Anything that I can do beyond A means I am successful.

Don't Let Success Make You Stop

Several years ago, I was speaking at a class of a good friend of mine, Dr. Brenda Lloyd Jones. I made the statement that I rarely ever use the word "success" about myself. Her response was, "You really should use the word 'success' about yourself, because you *are* successful. If you don't speak that you are successful, then you're *not* successful."

"You know, I don't use that term about myself," I replied, "because I think if I define myself as 'successful,' I will stop trying to get to where I am supposed to go. The moment that I believe that I am 'successful,' what reason do I have to get up in the morning?"

I start to think, *I am successful. Why do I have to keep pushing myself?* No, I believe I am truly successful because I have some new goal to reach, another corner to look around, another mountain to climb.

Success is not a destination that I reach where I can say, "I'm here. I'm done." Rather, it's a process in life. It is not that I say, "I've got it! I'm successful. I'm finished now." If you are "finished," where do you go from there? You have nowhere to go because you are "successful." No, success is ever changing. Today, success might be making sure my son achieves what he thinks he should. Tomorrow, success might be getting an e-mail from someone where our correspondence has been satisfying and productive. I think that "success" is forever changing, and that is why I am very careful in using that term about myself professionally. Most people tend to think that success resides in professional achievement. They rarely use it in terms of family life or about their personal happiness. "Success" has become almost a "term of endearment" for the business world. I ask, is that the only place that we can use the word "success"? Is that the only place where I can achieve success?

Success Is the Today that Leads to Your Tomorrow

No, it is not. We have so many potential areas to be successful in our lives, but I still use that term sparingly. For example, my son is eleven years old. He is still growing and developing. How do I know that today he is successful? What about his future? I might say that my marriage is "successful." Is it really? What happens five years from now? If it is a success today, can it become more successful over time? In my personal life, I view success as the process of trying to live my best life possible, not simply where I am at any given moment.

In terms of business, success is also not just an achievement. Instead, it consists of creating new strategies, setting new goals and finding new ways to make your business work. If I define success this way, then the life I lead as an African-American businesswoman is successful. It's not just "I achieved this, my name is on the door, I have that position." My staff has been helpful in my viewing success correctly. It doesn't matter what accomplishments I have or what award I just received; they still expect me to put all of that aside to come look at a patient's report, to examine a scan, to talk to a doctor. I don't get to "rest on my laurels," and that is why I love to come to work. Thanks to them, I can't live in what I did yesterday. I have to live in the now. I have to meet that new challenge, solve that new problem today.

Success doesn't reside in your past. No one cares that much what you did last week. No one cares what you did last Monday—more than likely they can't even remember it. Rather, true success is living in the moment, and it's moving down that road to get wherever it is you're going. People would say that I am successful. And with a new definition, I can agree. I am living in the now, experiencing the passion I have toward my business. It's fun for me. I love coming into the office and meeting the challenge that each new day brings. I'm constantly setting new goals, meeting them and moving toward that new mountain to climb, that new opportunity to achieve.

Entrepreneur 101 Takeaway:

Success is not a destination—it's a process. Keep that passion for your business that started you on the way. Success is living today fully—in the now—and turning each new corner on the road to where you're going.

CHAPTER 10:

Branding Yourself for Success

"Branding yourself" may be my favorite topic in this book. When I started this company ten years ago, I didn't know anything about branding. I had no idea that branding was a way to redefine both this company's image and my own, creating a recognizable and highly desirable and marketable package.

In 2002, I had been in business about four years and I was moving along steadily with my life, working hard, my attention focused on the task at hand. One day, I met with two women, Dr. Brenda Lloyd Jones and Yvonne Hovel of East Tulsa Dodge, to discuss ways of getting ahead in business. Yvonne Hovel and I were probably two of the most prominent African-American women in Tulsa, but we had no real public recognition. We were not making enormous strides in the business world—none of that existed ten years ago for African-American women—but we were both operating outside the norm, running multimillion-dollar companies almost in secret. We decided to meet once a month to find ways of becoming more socially connected. As African-American businesswomen ten years ago, we were not the "in" thing, not the "flavor of the month." We wanted to find a way to be noticed and set apart in the public eye.

Creating a Strategy

At our meeting, we discussed that one of my friends had been nominated for an award. I was still fairly new in the business world, and I had no idea that awards like this existed or how to make the social and business connections I needed. Where could we find this type of information? The three of us decided that each month we would pick up various local publications, including *Tulsa People* magazine, the *Oklahoman* and newspapers to find out what social events were taking place that we could attend, boards on which we could serve and awards we might win. I didn't know it yet, but I was about to learn what branding was.

The next thing I knew, my sister Doris called to tell me that the national magazine, *Black Enterprise,* was making awards to outstanding small business entrepreneurs. She wanted to nominate me. *Black Enterprise* is a national magazine where enormously successful African-American businesses receive exposure. I didn't really know what was involved, but I thought, *I am here in Oklahoma—sure, why not.* This was around Christmastime, she was spending the weekend at my house and we decided to go online to fill out the application for this award. We sent in some additional information, and a few months later, I received a letter from *Black Enterprise* notifying me that I was one of the finalists for Business Innovator of the Year, a national award.

This is incredible, I thought. *Here I am from Oklahoma, and I'm a finalist for a national award.* The event was held that year at

Gaylord Opryland in Nashville, Tennessee. No one knew who the winner would be—it was top secret, and what do you know—I won. I had come all the way from Oklahoma to win this national award, Business Innovator of the Year for *Black Enterprise*.

The speaker at the award ceremony was Cornel West, Professor of Religion and African-American Studies at Princeton University. After I received the award, I was photographed with Dr. West who told me that he was from Oklahoma and that when I went up on that stage to receive my award, I "looked good, walked good and talked good"—being from Oklahoma, that is! We were both country kids from Oklahoma, and he wanted to tell me he was proud that I represented our state so well because I looked good and I spoke well. That was definitely a high point for me!

They "Know You" Before They Meet You

When I returned to Tulsa, I began to see the value in winning such an important national award. The *Tulsa World* not only made a press release about my award, but wrote up a big story on me complete with pictures of this woman who had just won Business Innovator of Year for *Black Enterprise*. Following that, *Tulsa People* magazine wrote its own article and other publications began to pick it up. Ultimately, that award allowed me to win a million-dollar contract. I walked into a doctor's office, and the big four-page spread about my award in the *Tulsa World* business section was on his desk. Because he had read that article about my award, I was given a contract worth millions of dollars for HealthSouth Corporation. There was no marketing involved. Nothing I had done before gave me that kind of credibility and exposure.

I tell the story that every award I have on my wall represents a million dollars. That first award started me on the journey of branding myself; it taught me that image is everything. After the *Black Enterprise* award, I became a woman with a mission—to win more awards. First, I created a plan: I would gather all the weekly and monthly magazines and publications and look for events to attend and awards to win. I would find one and think, *I could go to this event—and I could win this branding award.* I had to do it this way, because I wasn't in the "in" crowd and I didn't have the inside information. However, I could read the papers and magazines. I tracked down awards and began to apply for them.

The next award I won was from *Tulsa People* magazine. In 2002, *Tulsa People* decided to recognize the fastest growing companies in Tulsa. I found this award in the *Tulsa People* business section, and I thought this was a real possibility. I applied for it, nominating myself. As part of the application, I had to give my financials; I decided right away that I had no problem doing this because the value of the award far outweighed making this disclosure. And once again, I won, receiving the *Tulsa People* award for Business Innovator just after winning for *Black Enterprise.*

What *Tulsa People* did for me and for my company has been nothing short of phenomenal. Now, I don't advertise with anyone other than *Tulsa People* magazine. Winning that award as Business Innovator for Tulsa did more for me than I could ever have imagined. Not only did I win that award, but each year I won other awards from *Tulsa People.* Each year, those awards got bigger, with *Tulsa People* spotlighting me and my business for the next four or five years. The second year, I didn't have to nominate myself; the magazine did it for me. That's when I realized how powerful an award could be. Everybody in Tulsa reads *Tulsa People*. I would walk into offices only to hear people remark, "You're the one in *Tulsa People!*"

Woman on a Mission—to Win!

Those awards marketed me. In places where I once could not even get an appointment, I was now walking in freely because my awards opened the doors. I was "branding" myself—setting myself apart from the pack, marking myself as a quality provider of health care with ready-made credentials. By now, I was looking to compete for as many awards as possible! And the next award I set my sights on was the Pinnacle Award. It had been advertised in both the *Tulsa World* newspaper and in *Tulsa People* magazine. When I learned of it, my response was, "Okay, showtime!"

I obtained an application packet, assembled my binder of information—including press releases on my previous awards—and submitted it. Once again, I won. And once again, coverage in *Tulsa World, Tulsa People* and other publications was simply enormous. Right there, I realized you can never pay for that type of recognition. Even an unlimited advertising budget won't bring you that recognition from others.

Awards of this caliber were actually my peers' golden "Seal of Approval." Once the *Tulsa World* had run an article on me, everyone in town knew who I was and what I was doing. At least once every month, I was in *Tulsa People*. What this coverage did for me was absolutely invaluable. I won numerous new contracts just because people had read about my little company. Those readers didn't necessarily know that I was the owner, but they knew that I was connected to it, I had won and they saw me as *a winner!*

I realized that I was onto something big because every award represented thousands and thousands of dollars of free press. I couldn't afford that—I was a small company. I didn't have an enormous advertising budget. What I did have was "me." I represented MCI. If I won an award, I might take home the plaque or statue, but MCI got the glory—and the new business. From that point on, I started winning every award for which I competed, and after I had won a number of them, opportunities for new awards just started to flood in. People would nominate me for awards, and I would win.

I learned how to brand myself—I became the instantly recognizable brand. In winning these awards, I also branded my company because my company itself won awards. I set the goal of winning two awards each year for ten years. I have only missed winning one award, and that was Woman of the Year for the State of Oklahoma. Although it was held in Oklahoma City—and living in Tulsa, I am an "outsider"—I still placed as one of the fifty most impressive women in the state. Once again, it allowed people who didn't know who I was to "know me." That "knowing me" translated into valuable contracts. This is why branding yourself is vital.

People are not necessarily going to remember you for yourself; however, win that award, and you and your company will become instantly recognizable. Once you're "branded," you'll find that you don't have to push as hard for advertising and recognition. As a result of all the awards I have won, I no longer need to attend that many events—but that branding has continued to make my company millions of dollars.

How You Can Brand Yourself

How can you brand yourself and your business? Start out just as I did. Pick up the local magazines and read the business section of the paper—that's where all those awards will appear. Find someone to nominate you. If you're a busy executive, you may not have a network of people nominating you for every award. However, you don't need that—award nominations can come by one woman or one man reading an article and deciding to put your name forward for an award. Once your name is known, you may have people you've never met know your reputation—your "brand"—and nominate you sight unseen.

I was in a meeting recently and spoke with a man I had never met before. I had been trying to explain to him who I was and why I thought that I could run his clinic. He told me that he already knew who I was. In fact, he had nominated me for an award four years earlier.

Begin to research what awards you can win. If you are in medicine, look for awards in your field. If you have a niche business (one that meets a small, specific need in your industry), stay focused on information about that area. Use the Internet, the newspapers and local and state magazines to find out what awards your field gives. Read press releases about other award winners. My field is medicine. I won the G.E. Award of Excellence for administrators for MCI Diagnostic Center.

Realize that you also have a learning curve when you begin to apply for awards. You may lose some of those awards because you're not familiar with the application process. I actually lost several awards when I first started. Although I won the 2007 award for Small Businessperson of the Year for the State of Oklahoma, I had applied for it once before in 2002. I still have the application packet that I sent in back in 2002—I think I kept it out of shame because my presentation was so elementary. There was nothing professional about that packet; I didn't have a clue as to what I was doing. The one that I submitted back then was about ten pages long. Today, my application package consists of over 100 pages. I learned to create the best possible application binder to present myself professionally.

Presentation Matters!

It wasn't just the binder that needed a more professional presentation. When I first began to win awards, I would just show up when I was to receive them. I keep several pictures of myself from those early awards on my wall to remind me that presentation is everything. The paper would call and tell me that they wanted to take a picture of me winning the award, giving me plenty of notice. Not once did I ever show up looking as if I were the successful woman who deserved to win that award. No, I looked like the woman who just got off that truck working all day. I look back now and laugh—I'm still proud of those awards, but I make a point of looking "picture perfect" these days. It's an important part of branding yourself.

Face it. When you're a woman, people expect you to be a successful businesswoman—but they frequently have an unconscious expectation that you will be beautiful and ladylike. Sometimes it's hard to combine that hard-driving businesswoman with the "total package." It has taken me eight years to get it right.

Now I make sure that I show up to award events looking like a success. I have a personal designer, a personal shopper, a makeup artist and a hairstylist on call for me.

How do I know that you have to be the total package? Two years ago, *Black Enterprise* called me and said, "We are looking for a woman who makes over a million dollars, is under forty and is attractive." Why couldn't she just make over a million dollars and be under forty? No one says, "We want a man under forty who makes a million dollars—oh yes, and he has to be drop-dead gorgeous!" However, when it comes to women, I have learned that the branding process often requires that we are not just smart, successful and articulate but beautiful as well. Now when I show up to receive an award, you won't ever have to worry about seeing me look like I just got off the truck. This was an important lesson I had to learn.

Think about it. A man is going to show up to receive an award in his best suit and a laundry-starched shirt complete with a coordinated silk tie. He may be wearing handmade shoes. His tie will have a perfect knot. His hair will be trimmed, and he'll be freshly shaven. For women, the standards are set even higher.

If you don't want to meet those standards; you won't get the recognition. I was telling my sister some time ago that if I hadn't done a "180" on my appearance, I don't believe I would receive the type of recognition I have today. I lost weight. I started traveling with people who are on call to help with my wardrobe, makeup and hair. You don't have to be "beauty-queen beautiful," but showing up looking your absolute best makes a huge difference.

When I first started out winning awards, trying to brand myself and MCI, I had three suits. I felt that no matter what, I could wear those suits to a business occasion, and I could count on them to make me look my best. I have several pictures of myself in them. None of them were tailored to me, but I didn't know the importance of that—that was part of my learning process. I keep those pictures to remind myself how far I've come in creating the "package" that brands me and MCI as unique and excellent.

Entrepreneur 101 Takeaway:

Branding yourself is vital to the survival of your company—and to your survival. Brand yourself by applying for every award possible for your company. Each award you win allows you to "meet" future clients without them ever having met you. Branding yourself will bring you press coverage you could never buy.

CHAPTER 11:

Redefining Yourself

I like the word "redefining." It describes a process that my company has gone through and continues to implement. Four years ago, we were trying to figure out "who" we wanted to be. We were Mobile Cardiac Imaging, and we were MCI Diagnostics, but we didn't have a tag line. We had nothing that really "defined" us and set us apart. One of the tasks—a contest, actually—that I gave my staff was to come up with a one- or two-word tag line for us, that explained who we were. My attitude was, "You are all part of this company, and we're in this together." One of my employees, Harley Davis, came up with the phrase "Redefining Diagnostic Imaging." That was perfect. That was what we were doing—redefining diagnostic imaging. We were doing something that no one else in this town had done.

As Harley was coming up with this phrase that redefined MCI, I was redefining myself at the same time. I was redefining who I was, what I had become and where I was going. "Redefining me" means that I don't believe that there is a day that goes by that there isn't something I could do differently, that the company could do differently to improve. I am quick to tell people that if it doesn't work, we are going to change it. And if it does work, we're going to make it better. That applies to the company, and it applies to me.

Be Constantly Aware of Ways to Improve

I am always on the lookout for the path to progress. To do that, I must welcome and embrace change. Rather than avoid change, I have decided that I am not too old and I am not too stagnated to "redefine me" at the drop of a hat. I can find something that doesn't work, and I can make it better. I can look at some aspect of the company, and I can say, "You know what? This process is no longer working. How do we make it better?" And it's the same with myself. I want to redefine myself so that I am ready for my best possible life. When should I redefine? Constantly.

One of the most important processes that I have learned to carry out, one which I have done now for nearly ten years, is that I redefine my company each year. Every December, I shut down everything that is not necessary, and I thoroughly examine all of my business processes. I am redefining the processes that we have in place now by capitalizing on what I have learned to make them better. That is redefining me as a businesswoman running MCI, and it is redefining this company.

In redefining myself and the company, I stay true to the original goal and intent of my business. In fact, "redefining" causes me to look at the ways we improve while remaining faithful to who I am, the purpose of the company, where are we going and what are we doing. You can't redefine something that hasn't already been defined. That's why you build a strong foundation of your real goals and mission for the company. Then, you can redefine by weeding out what is not working and fine-tuning the processes that are working but could be improved.

Redefining implies that I need to seek out change. I have to be willing to do business in a different way—whenever and wherever that is needed. First, you have to be able to see what changes need to be made. Second, you have to be willing to actually make those changes. Third, you have to have the ability to implement change, actually carry it out. If you can't accomplish these three steps, this is where you start getting into trouble in business. You not only have to be able to make changes, but you have to make them quickly. To redefine your business, you have to be a good decision-maker and be able to stand by the changes you have made. Remember, you and your business are in some ways separate, but in the end, as an entrepreneur, you and the business are joined together.

Redefining is key to survival and to the growth of your business. I learned that I had to redefine my appearance and presentation skills in terms of receiving awards that helped put MCI on the map. Likewise, I have learned to redefine the "way we do business" in order to make MCI a continuing, growing success.

Entrepreneur 101 Takeaway:

Change is part of life embrace the need to change yourself and your business practices in order to redefine and refine your business. Redefining keeps your competitive edge!

CHAPTER 12:

Be True to You

"Being true to yourself" is another key concept. I believe that part of my success is that I have never lost "me"—I have redefined "me," but I've never lost the essential self that I am. In many ways, I still am the same little country girl that I always was. I'm the same woman who laughs and jokes with her family, the same woman who is at times refined in my speech—and who occasionally lets the bad words slip out. I didn't lose me in the process. I have become better. I can look at myself and see that I have grown up with this company, become better with this company, but I have maintained me.

In Tulsa, in my business life, I'm Colleen. When I go back home, I am Lena. Nobody knows about all of this nonsense I do! My family is aware that I have become a somewhat successful woman, but I am not unapproachable. I never want to be considered unapproachable or the kind of person people can't talk to. When that happens, I think you start to lose who you are in the process. And how do you get "you" back? You might not ever be able to come back to who you are once the "you" gets lost. Today, I know exactly who I am. Sometimes people want to mess around with that. That's when I remind myself—and them, I know exactly who I am, and I know exactly who I am in this community. That confidence to stand my ground comes from keeping my identity as a person intact.

Know Who You Are and Act from That Core

I don't "hang out" a great deal. I don't know many people, but a very great many people know me. What I find interesting is that sometimes I can talk to people, and the whole time, they have some view of who I am that causes them to say something about me that I really didn't think they knew. I find myself thinking, *Did they Google me?* Those articles people pull up don't always reflect who I really am. If I don't have a strong sense of who Colleen really is—the real Colleen, not the one where I believe my own press—I can get myself in trouble in business. Fortunately, I'm not infatuated with my "image." My head is not inflated by some of my accomplishments or some of the accolades I have received.

My family has helped me not lose "me." My husband doesn't care what award I win, or how many times I get to meet important people. He's happy for me, but it's not that big a deal to him. What he does care about is if I come home and cook dinner! He cares that I still maintain the house. My son is the same way. He knows that Mommy is really busy, but he's not that impressed that I run a company. What he does care about is that if he needs a pair of tennis shoes or if he wants to go to the movies, I can take him there, that I'm fulfilling my responsibilities as his mother. What I do for my daytime job, my business meetings and the contracts I win don't matter that much to him. My family keeps me from "buying" my own image.

You Are Not Your Image

I know that image is out there; I have branded myself, and that's valuable, but I don't allow "the image" to penetrate who I am. If you buy that image and lose yourself, you will start living your life by what other people perceive of you. When you start to look through someone else's eyes, you see only what they see in you. It may not be the truth. Sometimes people have said, "I wish I were you." Who do they think I am? What would they do if they were me? Buy things? Go shopping all the time? Most of them don't know that some nights I go to bed at 3:00 or 4:00 in the morning, and I get up at 5:00. I work from sunup to sundown. I really don't have that much personal time.

Honestly, I don't get to sit here and eat bonbons all day! I have to work for a living. When you own a company, you take it home, you get up with it, and even before I get to work in the morning, I probably have taken ten or fifteen phone calls in my car on the way to work. I know the image that I have, but do I allow that to run my life? Even on a great day at work, I know that "image" is not reality. Knowing what is real and what is not is part of being grounded. As wonderful as the success is, you have to be able to divorce yourself from it on some level. You have to find balance. You have to know that when you are out on public display, you can't take that person home with you and live who "she" is twenty-four hours a day. You have to learn when to put her up. Keeping the "you" in you allows you to focus on what is important in your business, and what and who are important in your private life. It was the "you" who started on the path to success in business, and it's the "you" who will keep that success going.

Entrepreneur 101 Takeaway:

Stay grounded as the person you really are. Know that you have an image, but don't let it become your reality. Let the people around you help you keep your feet on the ground— and traveling the road to success.

CHAPTER 13:

Do You Have a Niche?

When I started my company, I was fortunate enough to find a niche—a distinct segment of market need that no one else was meeting. Did I realize that I had a niche? I don't believe I put it in those terms, but Mobile Cardiac Imaging (MCI Diagnostic Center) began with the idea of putting a nuclear medicine department on wheels. Had that been done before? Yes. Had it been done in Oklahoma? Yes, but not on the level that I envisioned. I took that concept of nuclear medicine on wheels, and I redefined it. One aspect of nuclear medicine that hadn't been made mobile was nuclear cardiology. There was a local company performing nuclear medicine "on wheels," but they were only doing general nuclear medicine.

What I did was to take the most complicated studies—myocardial perfusion scans and nuclear cardiology—and put them in a 55-foot van. In doing this, I developed a unique niche in the market because this type of mobile nuclear medicine hadn't been done within a 100-mile radius of Tulsa. What I did—and continue to do—was to develop an area that my competitors were not providing—or if they were providing it, to examine different and better methods. So, my niche was to put a diagnostic nuclear medicine department on wheels. Since I was already a nuclear medicine technologist, I decided to create a full diagnostic laboratory, making sure that it was accredited by the Nuclear Regulatory Commission, adding diagnostic treadmill equipment and a nuclear medicine camera. In addition, it had to have a "hot lab" where we could measure the amount and the type of radiation we gave to patients. We put it on wheels to take it to patients in outlying areas.

What Sets You Apart and Makes You Better?

In that first year, I put those plans together and made them a reality. When I developed the truck we use, I created a niche market. What we were doing just wasn't being done; I really didn't have any competitors in that arena. Having a niche market allowed me to set my company apart because I was doing something creative and "outside of the box." As I continued to build the business, I stayed within the medical area, but everything that I did from that point on was still a niche concept. The next year, I examined the idea of doing mobile ultrasound. Again, that was a niche because although mobile ultrasound already existed, I combined the two processes believing nuclear medicine and ultrasound go hand in hand. If the patient has a problem with the heart, more than likely there will be a need to do ultrasound. I put those two ideas together and said that if a patient is coming to us from a nuclear cardiac standpoint, we probably need to look at how well the heart is moving. Because I worked in this area, I realized that those techniques fit together.

I created a niche market by providing mobile ultrasound where we went out to rural areas and saw the patients there. These two niche markets that I met allowed me to set my business apart from the beginning. We differentiated ourselves from other people. We weren't just your "average" mobile nuclear medicine unit—in a real sense, our niche market helped in branding the business.

One of the very first awards that MCI won was Business Innovator for Tulsa, Oklahoma. Before MCI, who would have thought that you could put a nuclear medicine department on wheels and carry it out to both rural and urban areas? When you are trying to be creative as an entrepreneur, you want to do something that sets you apart, that is unique compared to what everyone else is doing. Even if they might have the same concept, what can you do to make yours different? There may be fifty car washes in town, but what makes your car wash better? Are you going to have a different kind of vacuum in it? Are you going to have blowers to push the water off the car? Will you use a special soap and wax combination to give a better finish?

I Wish I Had Thought of That!

The niche concept is significant; it allows your business to grow organically, without artificially trying to create a market because you are doing something no one else is doing. It gives your business an extraordinary advantage, and when others look at what you're providing, their response is, "Gosh! I wish I had thought of that." Look at some of the ingenious ideas that people have thought up—practically in their garages. Think of the woman who created Spanx® undergarments to give women a smooth silhouette under their clothing. No one else was doing that, and yet, what an obvious idea. It's the same thing that I did with nuclear medicine and mobile ultrasound. It was obvious, but no one was doing it.

As I continued to grow my business, I kept looking for those ideas that hadn't been done. The next niche market that I found was creating ultrasound staffing. In Oklahoma, we didn't have a company specifically set up to provide ultrasound staffing; back around 2000, ultrasound techs were hard to find. We had one school in Oklahoma that turned out something like twenty or thirty students at a time, but most of them were from out of state and headed back home. To find ultrasound and nuclear medicine technologists, I often had to go outside of Oklahoma.

I thought, *Why not hire enough ultrasound sonographers to allow me to staff the major hospitals in this area?* This was the beginning of my third venture, an ultrasound staffing company which eventually staffed St. Francis Hospital, Cancer Treatment Center, Tulsa Regional and Hillcrest. Soon, every major hospital in the general area was calling on this little company with just two rooms of office space to staff them. We were at St. Francis Hospital in Tulsa for about two years staffing them with technologists. Some days I would run two or three techs over there. At first, it filled a local market, but when word got out, it expanded from there. Many of my business ventures have been niches—and that is one reason they have all been very successful. I looked for a segment of the market that wasn't being filled, I applied my creativity to the situation and I created thriving businesses!

Entrepreneur 101 Takeaway:

Look within your business area for a need that is going unmet, for a market segment that is not being provided. Use your creativity to find a solution. Or take a current business, but offer a version that is different, better, unique. Let other people be the ones who say, "I wish I'd thought of that!"

CHAPTER 14:

The Art of Communication

Everyone communicates in some form or fashion, but does the entrepreneur communicate in a different way? Is there an entrepreneur communication style? I think that the art of communication for entrepreneurs is different most of the time and in most ways. It's a fact that 100 percent of all entrepreneurs like to hear themselves talk! Because of this tendency, it can be really difficult to listen to what other people have to say.

In addition, when you start your business, you have so many people pulling at you on any given day that you often can only give them a three- to five-minute window to tell you exactly what they need to say and then give them your response. Because of that time constraint, most entrepreneurs are going to talk quickly. We have so much to say, and other people have things they want to say to *us*. When you're running a small business, you have a great deal to focus on in addition to getting your point across. How can you say what you need to say, hear what you need to hear—and keep your business going?

What Is Not Being Said?

I think that other people give more credence to what small business entrepreneurs have to say than we do ourselves. Because you have a business, people often think you have a magic key to success. Although they often want to hear what you have to say, they also frequently want you to listen to them. It is key for an entrepreneur to be able to listen to what others are saying and how they are saying it. Our communication is not limited to accurately giving out information. I have found that listening is vital because it is not what people actually say most of the time that matters— it's what they don't say.

Because this is a society of e-mails, text messages and business over the Internet, we lose the nonverbal cues from face-to-face communication. I find that what I really need to know is typically what people *don't* say in that e-mail. For example, if you send me a business e-mail, I am going to read it two or three times. Are you telling me, yes, you have the contract just show up and it's yours? Or are you telling me that I *might* have that contract, but I still have to work to earn it? The subtle cues that let me know which one you are telling me are lost in an e-mail or a text message.

I have learned in business communication that most of the time, it is not that you want to hear me, but rather you want *me* to hear *you*. I constantly challenge myself when people are talking to me to listen and not say anything. For the most part, you really don't want to hear what I have to say; you want me to hear you. Sometimes, you want me to hear your ideas. I have had those conversations where people are talking to me while I'm biting may tongue trying not to say anything because it will be inappropriate.

Frequently, people really don't want to hear what you have to say, and they don't want the truth.

When It's Better Not to Speak

To counteract this, I have started telling people that I am always honest. By that I mean that it's likely that I am going to tell you something that you don't want to hear! Often, I have an internal struggle to be quiet and listen because you really don't want me to say what I really think. I am probably pitched business ideas every other day. Do those people honestly want me to tell them what I think of their business idea? No, they don't, but I also know that hearing positive or negative feedback and hearing explanations as to why this does or does not work are also what people need. Sometimes there is a struggle inside me. It's like being in a classroom, and you constantly want to raise your hand. Knowing you can't do that all the time, you'll raise your hand only to feel a "magical force" pull it back down. Some of my conversations are like that. I want to tell the person the truth, but I have to restrain myself, thinking, *Don't say anything. Please don't say anything or this conversation will end in a way you won't like.* I just listen, and we part on friendly terms.

Sometimes if I say what I really think without my disclaimer that I am always honest, I can be offensive. When I tell people that I am always honest, I explain that it means I am about to tell them something they may not want to hear. I am going to tell them anyway because they asked. So I might say, "Maybe that is not a good idea, but you know what? When it comes to business ideas, it doesn't matter if it I think it is a good or bad one. It is your idea, and what matters is what your heart tells you. If your heart says pursue it, then pursue it." Listen to the good, the bad and the ugly and at some point, you, the entrepreneur, need to hear all sides of it.

For an entrepreneur, the art of communication is probably the most important skill that you can develop. When I first started in business, I was a technologist making about $40,000 to $50,000 a year, but I was attempting to do business with people who were making millions of dollars. Obviously, we were not on the same socioeconomic scale. I didn't have too much in common with my potential clients. They had already "arrived," and in trying to deal with them, I needed to appear as if I was somewhere in the same arena as they were. I needed to appear as if I was some-where close to where they were because the gap between us was so significant. If you can't bridge that socioeconomic gap, you can't communicate.

Learn to Find the Common Ground with Anyone

People who are successful like to be heard as well, and you want to listen! As a good entrepreneur, you are going to listen because you are sitting in that client's office, trying to get that business. They have the business for you, but the socioeconomic gap between you makes for a struggle. You are not "there" finan-cially, but you have to look and act as though you are. That's difficult because anytime that you start a small business, you are not going to have the funds up front. You need to appear as if you are financially well off because no one is going to give business to the person who looks like they can't pay the next light bill! In addition to making the best appearance you can, how do you bridge those gaps?

When I first started my business, I was in an environment where I dealt mostly with men. Almost all of the hospital administrators were men, and when I walked into the room, it was typically full of men. That was another gap. Was I going to be making small talk about taking a cooking class? About my son? No, I was in with men—that's not what they talk about. I had to figure out what they wanted to talk about and it seemed to be sports. Early on, I wasn't the greatest conversationalist about sports, but I became one.

I don't even like sports, but I began watching enough to know who was playing and what was significant so I could bridge that communication gap with businessmen. If you are in a room with someone who has a different hobby, you need to ask yourself if that's something you can talk about. Did I do my homework on people beforehand? Yes, but often there was no homework I could do. I met people so high up on the totem pole that nobody in my little group knew them. However, I think that what makes a good entrepreneur is the same quality that makes a good marketing person—the ability to talk with anyone. I always say that I had to market my company early on. In addition to the many hats that I wore, I was also the marketer. I am by far not the best marketer, but I marketed my company myself early on because I had no choice. The moment that choice opened up, however, I hired a marketer.

I want the marketer who is there to hear what needs to be heard and be able to talk with anybody. There are no racial barriers, no color barriers and no gender barriers with them. That is what makes a good marketer and a good communicator. They are the person who walks into a room and is assertive in finding that common ground with other people.

As an entrepreneur, you have to be varied enough in your personality that you think, *I might not be an expert on this, but I have an opinion.* Having an opinion and being able to talk *and* listen are what carry you through. You can develop the ability to listen and to find that common ground!

Entrepreneur 101 Takeaway:

Learn to listen to what is being said and what is not being said in any communication, and then learn to find the common ground with the people with whom you do business. Be well read, observe and figure out what interests them. You can learn to talk with anyone!

CHAPTER 15:

The Competitive Edge—What's Yours?

As an entrepreneur, you need to learn what your competitive edge is in whatever you are marketing and whatever qualities make you better than your competition.

Several years ago, I went to a meeting where a man asked me, "Why would I want to send my patients to you? There are a number of diagnostic imaging places. Why are you different?" In so many words, he was trying to find out what my competitive edge was.

I had to really think about that. After being in business almost ten years, I thought that I knew what set MCI apart. Honestly, however, I didn't, and I had to identify those factors. I knew I had a competitive edge—that was why so many doctors were sending their patients to us. But how do I put that competitive edge into a precise, definite statement when someone corners me in a room and asks why they should choose my business over my competitors? I came back home and identified my competitive edge.

Put It Into Words—and Sell It!

My competitive edge was that I not only created one of the most beautiful centers in our arena, but we had an extremely rapid turnaround with patients. We schedule patients within four hours of receiving the referral We had the report transcribed and faxed to the doctor's office within twenty-four hours, if not sooner. Additionally, we would send a confirmation allowing the doctor to know that we have scheduled his patient. Those four items comprised my competitive edge. None of my competitors were doing that. I began to capitalize on those attributes of our business once I realized that I had that edge. I knew that our business was different and better, but I had just never put it into words.

Once I had identified it, I sold my competitive edge. I approached potential clients saying, "These are the things that we do better than anybody else. No hospital in town can compete with me. I can get your patients in faster, I can get your report back in twenty-four hours." Actually, I can get it back in almost two hours! I knew that I had facets of my business that made it better, but when I identified and communicated that competitive edge, it was like I had bottled and packaged my company.

There had been no question that I had an edge over my competition, but I needed to define it to myself so that I could communicate it to others. It became a selling point of our services. It wasn't just that we were a clinic because there were clinics all over town. I had to figure out what made us better, and how we grew to be the biggest when we were the last ones to enter the game. Once I identified the answer to that question—once I could put it into words and speak it—I could market our company. I could say, "This is what we do that is better than any of the competition."

I sold that package to my staff, and they bought in because now they knew exactly what that competitive edge was. When people approached them with that same hard question that this one man approached me with, they knew the answer. Being able to identify, speak and communicate our competitive edge branded us and tagged us as a company set apart by excellence and innovation. We were able to bottle and sell MCI with greater assurance than ever knowing that we offered a service no one else did.

Entrepreneur 101 Takeaway:

Examine your business. What makes it different and better than your competition? This is your competitive edge. That competitive edge bottles, packages and sells your business for you. Find it. Identify it. Put it into words. Speak it. It's the answer to the hard question, "Why should I do business with you?"

CHAPTER 16:

Your Management Style—What Is It?

Management style is developed over time. I don't believe that any manager wakes up one morning and says, "I have it. I have the perfect management style. I look good, I dress great and I talk well. That is my style." It doesn't happen that way. Your management style—the way you handle people and your business—develops as you grow with your business. When I first started my business, my management style could best be described as "crisis management." I was a crisis manager.

A crisis manager reacts to each crisis as it comes along, and when you are starting your business, life itself is a crisis. Every single day is a crisis. For the first several years, I worked as a crisis manager. This meant that I wasn't proactive—I was reactive. I didn't act—I reacted. As I began to own the several companies that I have today, my management style started to develop because I began to learn about myself. I am an aggressive female—and the truth is that African-American females are usually seen as being aggressive in business, and I think that women in general are considered aggressive in business. We are labeled quickly.

A Woman Manages Differently Than a Man

As an African-American woman in business, I found that I had to learn how to talk to my staff. As a woman, I needed to be almost motherly. As a mother, if you discipline your children harshly, they get mad at you, whereas if their father is somewhat harsh, they tend to forget it. I realized that if a man owned my company, he could afford to be gruff with the employees or not even speak to them, and it would be okay. Early on, I learned not to shut my office door. If I did, it gave the impression that I was angry when all I was trying to do was communicate that I needed to get some work done. Sometimes I just wanted to say, "Look, since my door is open all day long, you guys never leave me alone. I can't get any work done!" But my employees never took that closed door to mean that.

I read an interesting book about six years ago. This book said that for every time an employee interrupts you, they take an average of seven minutes. Then, it takes you fifteen minutes to get back on track. With twenty-six or more employees, that meant that I never got anything done! Due to that, I stayed at work until 8:00 or 9:00 P.M. because the greatest part of my work is accomplished between 5:30 and 8:00 P.M., once the employees have gone home.

During this time, I learned something. In terms of trying to define who I was in my management style, I had to look at how I addressed my employees. I went from a crisis manager to being an aggressive manager to learning how to manage without trampling on the feelings of my employees.

I found that I needed a barrier between the employees and me. If anything bad happens to them, I am not the bearer of that bad news. They have a supervisor to do that, although because I am a hands-on manager, nothing in my company happens without my knowing it. I don't know if my employees have all figured that out, but it is true. My management style has changed from reactive to proactive. By a proactive management style, I mean that I constantly am looking at ways we can change how we operate in order to be more efficient and provide better service.

One thing I cannot change is trying to manage from a distance. When you own a small business, you are the "owner on site." There is a different relationship that has developed due to the fact that I am on site. Out of the twenty-six employees we have, only two of my employees have ever worked in a company where the owner was there every day. That relationship of being able to talk with the owner directly can be beneficial to your employees and to you, but it can also be a hindrance. Everyone wants to talk to you, and you have a level of personal contact that changes your management style.

I believe that at this point in my life, being on site and having close contact with my employees allows me to be both a reactive and a proactive manager. I react to the various situations that come up, but I am also able to be proactive concerning the future and management of the company. This close personal contact also allows me to really know the people I have working for me, what their strengths and weaknesses are and what their capabilities are.

Expect Your Style to Develop and Change

I am not the manager today that I was ten years ago. Your management style changes and develops over the years. I have more balance in the various roles I have to carry out as a manager. Today, I find that I don't necessarily have to say a great deal to my staff because early on I hired adults who didn't need constant supervision. I try to operate with that as a goal, but I am also aware that employees will be employees. They are human and imperfect, and due to that, there are disciplinary actions that you still have to carry out.

One good thing that I have developed with my management style of being both proactive and reactive is that while I will tell you what is wrong so you can correct it, I will also let it go once the issue is settled. I can't carry a grudge, I can't be upset with you and I can't be angry with you because if I am, I will end up carrying you home with me—and I just can't afford to do that. This is already an 8:00 to 8:00 job. At 8:01 P.M., I need to walk away. I never carry any feelings of anger toward any employee. I need to be able to go off the clock at the end of the day. Learning to do this is one of the ways my management style has developed over the years.

One part of developing your management style is being flexible for where you and your business are at any given time. Because I have had to grow into my own management style, I have had to consider what type of manager I want to be. Am I a fair manager? Yes. Am I a stern manager? Yes. Am I a manager with an aggressive personality? Yes. I learn to keep those qualities in balance, and I find that despite changing situations, there is rarely an occasion that I have to pull out the "hard sides" of my managerial style. Many of my employees have been with me for a while, and they have come to understand my managerial personality. They know what is expected of them, and they know if they don't perform, then "she" will be coming after them. Do the job so "she" doesn't have to come!

Entrepreneurial 101 Takeaway:

Your style as a manager develops over time. You grow and change as an individual, and so does your business. Find what works for you, the size of your business and the employees you have, remembering that as your style is established, your employees learn what is expected of them and how to flow with you.

CHAPTER 17:

Entrepreneurship 101—The Basics

When people first decide to go into a business, do they get to start out as a "real" entrepreneur? No, they don't. That comes with the opening of the "glass ceiling" where you know you will succeed. From the day that I began in business, I never had the thought in my head that I wasn't going to succeed. At the same time, I never had dreams of sitting in this chair today. I believed that I was where I was, and while I didn't believe that I was going to fail, I knew that if the worst happened, I still had something that I could go back to. I could always return to being a nuclear medicine tech. Part of the true entrepreneur spirit is that if you fail, you can begin again with whatever it was that you had before your business. You can go back to where you started.

Don't Fear Failure and Don't Quit

Because I knew that I could always start over, I never had that crippling fear that I couldn't make it. Frequently, you read stories of great entrepreneurs who had ten or fifteen companies. How could they do that? They never had that fear of failure. If you never have that fear of failure, you can always get back up. If one company doesn't survive, then another might. True entrepreneurs are not quitters, and they don't give up. You can't be afraid of failing. Every day in a small business, failure is just one step away. You can either take one step forward or one step back. Always take that one step forward—and the fear will tend to leave you.

When you are making $50,000 a year, and you buy a truck for almost a million dollars, that can produce pressure and fear. I have done those things—I'm not afraid. I remember having a conversation with my banker once where he asked me, "Do you ever get afraid?" Of what? Failure? No, because I believe that as long as I push, I can do it. I work hard, I work long hours and I don't have that fear of losing anything. If I did it once, then I believe I can build it again. The true entrepreneur has no fear of failing because they can't lose what they started out with—and they can't lose what they are.

That doesn't mean that the entrepreneur doesn't have to deal with the possibility of failing. You never get there, you never get to the point to where you don't have those thoughts about failure. As long as there is competition, as long as the title of your company has "business" in it, then you have to deal with that possibility. Business is volatile. Anything can happen. It is just like life; every day is a different day. Every day has a different sunrise and a different sunset. Business is like that.

Can I wake up tomorrow and know exactly what is going to happen? No, I can't. Today I can walk in to work and think I have my day planned. Then, two of my biggest vendors walk in off the street and decide to pay a surprise visit. I don't know when I get up in the morning what is going to happen during my day—no entrepreneur can get up and say, "Today is going to be a perfect day." You never know what the day will bring.

You can't let the fear of failure ruin you. You can't get around the possibility of things going wrong. This is part of how you live as an entrepreneur. You have to "do your time." Every day people face different fears. They face different goals to accomplish, different mountains to climb. What happens is that one day you wake up and say, "I am not afraid of losing anything. I am not quitting and I am not afraid of not getting there. I am doing my time." At some point you realize that you are going to keep at it, you have accomplished one goal, faced one obstacle and you can face more. There's no switch to turn on and off. You have to decide that fear of failure is not going to be what runs you.

Don't Let Fear Run You Out of Business

Fear cannot be your focus because that is what makes people quit business. I don't think that there is anybody who has done business and who became a multimillionaire without having something that went bad. Life just doesn't work like that. You have obstacles, and you make your call on how to get past them. I was reading in the paper about the December 2007 ice storm and power outages in Tulsa. There were people who lost power for over a week. One business owner had $6,000 worth of meat in his freezer, and his business was already on the edge. He made a call to donate all the food that he had in his store to a shelter because he had no power. Within twelve hours, his power came on, but he made a conscious decision that put him out of business.

Would I have made that decision? No, I wouldn't have. I would have waited the twelve hours. I would have bought a generator, but those are the decisions that you make. Are you tough enough to stay or will you quit? That man's business hadn't been operating for even a year. Face up to the fact that the first year is tough, and the second year may be tough, too. For me, all my years were tough up until somewhere between my fifth and seventh year when that glass ceiling opened up, and I knew that it was going to be okay. Today we are a multimillion-dollar company, and very few women-owned businesses make it to the multimillion-dollar level. It takes toughness to stay!

Entrepreneur 101 Takeaway:

What separates the true entrepreneur from the ones who quit is the ability to stop fearing failure. Know that whatever you brought into your business, you can take away with you. Get tough and refuse to be controlled by fear.

CHAPTER 18:

Rules of Engagement for Entrepreneurship

I have ten "Rules of Engagement" that I live by as an entrepreneur—I patterned my rules after those of Sam Walton of Wal-Mart. They worked for Sam, and they work for me.

Rule # 1: Commit to your business. You want to believe in your business more than anything else. If you love your work, you will be out every day trying to do the very best that you can. Soon everyone around you will catch the passion and the fever of your business.

Rule #2: Share your profits. Give back to the people who are making you what you are. If you don't give back to those people—your employees—they won't stay with you. Do you penny-pinch, or do you give back to the community and share some of your success? I have offered my staff the chance three times to buy stock in this company. I gave them this opportunity because I believe that I didn't get here by myself.

Rule #3: Motivate the people around you. If you set standards and goals, people will try to meet them. I see that with my clinics and with the people who work for me. They are living at the standard that I set. That is why I rarely ever come to work sick—that is, where anyone knows that I'm sick! If I am sick, everybody around me gets sick because as an owner you set the tone for the daily environment.

Rule # 4: Communicate everything you possibly can. It does not do you or your business any good if you are the only one with all of the information. There is not anything that I know that would assist in running my company that I don't tell. I am going to tell you how to manage. I am going to tell you how to make the best decisions. Every person in my company is in some management capacity; I want them to make the decisions that I would make if I wasn't here for some reason. I tell them to ask themselves, "What would Colleen do?" If they can answer that correctly, then we are in good shape. If they make the decision that *they* would make, they need to be reminded that this isn't their company—they don't get to make their own decisions concerning this company. I tell them, "You make the decisions that you believe that I would make because you know what I believe." I have made really good decisions with this company and as long as I believe that, I will insist that my employees make the same decisions I have made.

Rule #5: Appreciate your staff. Appreciate their levels of success. Rejoice with them in the levels of success that they reach in their professional and personal lives. When you do that, you are free to be who you really are with your staff. And your staff likes to be appreciated! I have always said that if I didn't work at this company, I would want to work here because, first of all, I am a tech myself, and I've made this company "tech friendly." My techs have different bonus structures for different times of the year. I do all sorts of different things in my office—at any given point, they might receive an envelope just for appreciation. We have special appreciation lunches, we "do Christmas" and I try to create various ways to make this center work for them. I am not going to say that I am the easiest manager to work for because I didn't get here being the most lighthearted person. I handle business, but I don't micromanage my employees. As a result, we don't have a great deal of turnover. In ten years, I think we might have had maybe ten or fifteen people who have left. Our employees want to stay with us!

Rule # 6: Listen to everyone in the company. Just because someone is the janitor doesn't mean that he doesn't have an opinion worth hearing. Why do I listen to everyone and try to honor the value in their comments? I didn't get here with them, and I probably won't leave here with them, but I believe you are going to tell me something that you believe is valuable for our company. Because I want to listen, I have an open-door policy so that I can hear what you want to tell me. If you have something to tell me, you can believe that I am going to listen. I may not use it, but you have the opportunity to tell me. If your idea makes sense, then we are going to change what we're doing. I listen to my staff, to the people on the front line who actually talk with the customers, the ones who see the patients, the employees who talk with the doctors. What you have to say becomes part of the circle of what we're doing here. You have the potential to make this a better company—so you can be sure I'm going to listen to you.

Rule # 7: Give more than people expect. This goes right back to our competitive edge. We give our clients, our customers and our doctors not only what they want but more than they expect. Whenever you do this, you operate in a place of strength. Do we do this all of the time? Maybe not. But 95 percent of the time, I believe that we exceed our customers' and our patients' expectations from the moment they walk in the door. That is why I am concerned about how you are greeted when you come to the facility and how you are spoken to on the phone. Even though all of those things might seem petty for an owner to concern herself with, this is how I got here, and this is how I am going to stay here.

Rule # 8: Watch how other people spend your money. Control your expenses. You want to look at your expenses from your competitor's standpoint. You always want to find that competitive edge where you can save money and provide better service.

Rule # 9: Be very effective at marketing who, what and why you are. Market absolutely everything that makes your business significant and unique. Remember, that is your competitive edge—use it to sell your business to your clients.

Rule # 10: Always try to swim upstream. When you swim upstream, you can ignore the "conventional wisdom" of everyone else as to how they are doing business. You are marching to the beat of your own drum, and you are not following the norm. When I first got into business ten years ago, I wasn't the first mobile ultrasound company and I wasn't the first staffing company. I competed with an established company for months even though they didn't do a good job. They didn't show up, leaving the patients hanging with no help. They would cancel thirty minutes before they were supposed to arrive or they simply wouldn't show up. They didn't get the reports back in a timely manner. Even though we weren't doing any of those things, we couldn't catch a break. I was competing with a monster because even though this company was not providing quality care, it had the business. When you already have the business, a new competitor can show up, but it doesn't make any difference. Often, the clients can't see the forest for the trees. They have a provider already, and they're not interested in you.

Don't Try to Get New Results with the Same Methods

I competed with one certain company for somewhere between six months and a year. I heard how much clients disliked this company and how they wanted things to change, but not one of those hospitals changed over to us. I spent a year chasing the business. Finally, I changed my whole way of marketing. It didn't matter how badly this other company did business, they had been there for ten years. They had longevity on their side. People would call me to talk with them. I would run out and talk with them thinking, *Okay, you know that they are not a quality health care provider. Certainly you will give me your business.* No, it didn't work that way. They were familiar with this other company. When you have familiarity, it is hard to move away from it to the unknown. After a year of chasing all of these hospitals that wouldn't change over to us, I stopped. As long as I was playing the game, swimming in the same direction and chasing and fighting for business, I never got it.

How did I swim upstream? I stopped chasing that business. Instead, I concentrated on making my business better, and when I did that, I made a place and a name for myself in the marketplace. I changed the direction I was putting all my energy. I did something different and it paid off. This other company didn't show up.

They were never on time. Their equipment was broken. I had brand-new equipment and a brand-new van, but none of that mattered because they were on their home turf, and it was familiar to those hospitals. I stopped and I swam the other way. In six months, all of that business came my way. As long as I was chasing it and fighting it, I didn't get a single client. I went out and made new business and eventually, the others came.

My mobile ultrasound competitor had been in business for a long time and had become sloppy. They had become complacent because they were the only ones in business with no competition. They thought they didn't have to show up on time. People take off their jobs in these rural areas only to have the mobile ultrasound unit not show up. All of these rural communities didn't know that there was another option. We, however, concentrated on the business we did have, and we made it the best possible. Suddenly, we found that one hospital administrator knew the next one, and the next one knew the next one, and so on. Eventually all of that business that I spent a year chasing came my way, and that was because I chose not to continue to swim downstream. I started to swim upstream by making our business the best possible. Finally, thanks to this change in mindset, we were the ones in the driver's seat.

Entrepreneurial 101 Takeaway:

When you follow these ten proven rules for engagement in your business, you position yourself to receive the success you have earned.

CHAPTER 19:

Entrepreneurship— A Life of Sacrifices

The entrepreneur's sacrifice is tremendous. Initially, we all have dreams of grandeur, thinking, *I will be able to work for myself and nobody will tell me what to do. I'll get to go home. I won't have to go to the office. I will have so much money.* Surely in this day and age, no one still believes in this fairy tale! In every book on being an entrepreneur, the first story you read will tell you that this dream is not real! You are going to work longer and harder than anyone else, you are going to have more hats to put on than anyone, you are going to get paid less than anyone in your company and you are not going to get to go home early. On any given day, you are not even going to get to be your own boss.

When you start out, you have thousands of "bosses"—every person you are doing business with or who walks through your door is your boss. The fantasy of being your own person does not exist. The sacrifices you have to make, however, really do exist.

But I'm My Own Boss Now!

One of the reasons so many businesses fail is because the expectations that new entrepreneurs have are faulty. They are wearing the rose-colored glasses of their dreams, and what they really need are a pair of clear glasses to see reality. The biggest sacrifice is family. As women entrepreneurs, we still are required to do all of the things we did before. You still have to cook dinner. If you have children, you still have to go home to take care of them and be sure they do their homework and get to bed. You still have to do the laundry. Even if you are fortunate enough to have help, you will still sacrifice time with your family.

When I started this company, my son was six months old and I was going through a divorce. It was just the two of us. Fortunately, I knew a great family—the Reeds—who helped take care of my son. I would be stuck in some little town, and they would pick him up and take care of his needs. They took daily care of him during his early years, starting when he was just an infant.

I had just gotten the company off the ground when he was about three or four. I remember days that I would drive the rig up to his day care. All of the women there knew me. I would call on the phone to tell them that I was coming through and to have him ready because the truck was too big to park. It was just like driving a semi to the day care, and they would bring him out to the street where I had stopped traffic and then climb up to the truck to give him to me.

Even Your Children Sacrifice

I don't know if my son remembers those days or not, but when we would go to the office, he'd start to cry, "Mommy, no!

Mommy, no!" because he knew that there wouldn't be anything for him to do or any toys to play with. He knew that we would be at the office for some time. That was a major sacrifice for both of us. I built my new office with him in mind. He could stay at the office and watch television on a plasma screen, or work out in a specially equipped room. Time with him was the biggest sacrifice that I had to make because no matter how many times he said, "Mommy, no!" I still had to go to work. People have wanted me to have constant regret about the life that I chose and how I pulled his life into my life. They have wanted to point out the sacrifices my child had to make.

I have had to get way beyond the sacrifice of my child for the good of what I have done for people and the good that I have done for my life. At the end of the day, my son has a great life—he's a great young man, and he has done very well. Would I have done anything differently? No, I wouldn't. Even now, my family still makes sacrifices because I am here at this office so many evenings until 8:00 P.M. However, the bonus is that my son is now eleven-and-a-half years old, my husband works with the company and we all go home together. There is rarely a day that we don't leave this office together. I know that if I stay here until 7:00 P.M., my guys are doing just fine. My son actually has his own office so he can work on homework or whatever he needs to do. From that standpoint, I have no regrets about my choice. When I gave my speech for winning the award for Small Businessperson for the State of Oklahoma, I called him up on stage. It was good for him to hear me share that story of the sacrifices we both made when he was little. I thanked him for letting me achieve the goals that have benefited us all.

Family sacrifices are huge; men generally have someone at home to pick up the slack of running a household. My husband is a wonderful help, but he's not a great cook! For a male entrepreneur, a wife is wonderful. He can go out, work all day and have that support at home. He doesn't have to worry about picking up the kids and going to the grocery store and doing all of the domestic things that women tend to do. My husband and my son don't care what I have done during the course of my day or what accolades I have received. I still have to cook, I still have to clean my kitchen and I still have to do the things that come with being a wife and a mother. Do you always have the time and energy to take care of yourself? No, you don't.

Where Is All That Money?

Part of the entrepreneur fairy tale is that you are going to have so much extra time because you are not working for "the man." You soon find out that you have become "the man." If you have enough guts to go out and start a business, then you have to work harder for "the man" that you are because if you don't, you will have to go out and work for a real "the man" because you didn't put the time, energy and dedication into working for yourself.

I implore everyone with the entrepreneur idea to listen to this advice. Do your research. I don't know anyone who has started a business that said, "I got to work the hours I wanted. I was happy all the time, and life was good." I really am what some people call a workaholic, but I have no regrets for having that label attached to me. I gave my energy at the beginning, and I still continue to do that after almost eleven years. As long as you love and enjoy what you're doing, you have the passion to give your best, but it does cause conflicts. You have to weigh going out of town or working, and you always believe that the business is the most important entity. If there is no business, then there are other problems that are created.

I think that any entrepreneur who starts a business needs to be well-balanced. By that, I mean that in addition to being a successful entrepreneur, you need to have something outside your business that you enjoy. I believe that a hobby or some other form of passion makes people well-rounded. Unfortunately, I don't have a hobby. I tried to find something I could enjoy so I took a cake decorating class thinking that would give me something that I could enjoy. I enrolled in the class and attended it. I bought every tool possible, not realizing that a hobby grows with you over time. You don't "do it" all in a day.

I've also tried collecting the right shoes and gave it up when someone noticed my collection and asked how long I had been collecting. I answered that I had been collecting for a couple of weeks. Once again, I tried to "accomplish" my hobby in a day. I haven't bought a shoe since because I tend to treat the hobby like I do business. Get it done, get it done now. As a result, I am still waiting to enjoy that part of life!

Money becomes a huge sacrifice because you first have the misconception that you are going to have so much money. If you have employees, you pay them first. In fact—and I don't advise this—early on I thought, *I own the business. Why take money? It's all mine at the end of the day.* For years, I was the lowest paid employee in my company. Whenever I needed money, I knew that I had it. So until 1996 or so, I made $56,000 a year. I took draws that compensated for that salary, but I didn't pay myself correctly and that is a big mistake that entrepreneurs make. I knew that I could pay myself, but I just didn't need the money. When I started this company, I had no debt. I had a house. The cars I traded every year—I paid for them because I didn't know any better. I figured all the money went to one place. Finally, I learned better.

In 2006, I had a really good banker who asked me, "Colleen, where is your money? Where is the money that you pay your-self?" He just started to laugh, looking at my financial state-ments. "Colleen, you may own it all, but you need to pay yourself." I respect him highly, and from that day, I started to pay myself a salary.

Why do I need to pay myself? For financial freedom. It makes a huge difference because somewhere down the line, not paying yourself really makes a difference. I went to buy a brand-new Mercedes, and I saw the car that I wanted on the showroom floor. I knew that I had money to buy it, but I didn't "look the part" that particular day—and "looking the part" is always important. The salesman I was working with must have figured that if this woman comes in here and says she wants this car, she must be able to buy it. We had to move about six or seven cars to get this car off the floor, and here I was with one of my friends, dressed casually. I knew I could afford it, but when I went to buy that car, I was told that I had so many vehicles and so much "stuff" under my name that I needed to sell something. I thought, *Which one?* Those were all business mobile units, but according to my income, I didn't make enough money. I was *worth* enough money, but I didn't *make* enough. I knew that I could afford that car, but you have to be worth it on paper. That was the significance of increasing my salary. If I am worth so many million dollars but I only make $100,000, my salary doesn't reflect what I'm worth. Worth determines what I can do. It determines not just buying a new Mercedes, but getting that loan at the bank for the business.

As a small business owner, the credit worthiness of the business was *my* credit worthiness. Even though I finally was "making all that money," failure to pay myself put me in the position of not having the financial freedom I needed to run my company.

Entrepreneur 101 Takeaway:

Be prepared for the tremendous sacrifices you will make in terms of time, energy, family life and money. Count the cost before you start so you remain in the business you worked so hard to begin.

CHAPTER 20:

Banking Entrepreneur-Style: What Your First Banker Didn't Tell You

This is the most important chapter to me because when I started this company ten years ago, I didn't have any business relationships and I didn't know the importance of or the "how- to's" of having a business banking relationship. When I first started my company, I didn't go to the banks because I didn't have any money. I didn't have enough money to buy a $654,000 truck. My understanding of a bank was that you had to have money to borrow money. When I was trying to borrow money for the truck, people steered me to financing companies instead of a bank.

This is where most entrepreneurs suffer. If you don't understand how banks lend money, you could have the best idea in the country and not be able to finance it. If you have no bank relationships and you are not established, banks will not give you enough money to walk off the street as a tech and buy a $654,000 truck. I knew how to pay my personal bills, but I didn't know how to run my company financially. I had a business plan because the bank wanted to see where we were going. I no longer deal with banks that want a business plan from me—I know where I want to go, but I don't have the external pressure of the business plan mapping out where I'm supposed to be in five years.

There was so much the banks didn't tell me. First, they didn't tell me that there really wasn't any "free" money out there for me. Second, they didn't tell me that because I didn't have a track record of being successful, they weren't going to take a chance on me until I proved I could do it on my own. Instead, the bank is going to ask you if you have parents, relatives or friends with money you can borrow. They are going to route you to everybody else for you to borrow money. Every time you are routed to someone else, you have to give up a piece of what you believe your dream is. Have you come all that way to give up this dream? To have the banker tell you that you have no proven record of success with this venture? Then the bank asks if you have checked with minority business groups and the Small Business Administration. They won't tell you that there really is little chance of getting money there, and if you do get some, you will work yourself into a knot trying to get $5,000, which is not going to last you a day.

I Needed a Banker to Do More Than Just Take My Money

If the banks won't tell you these things, what do you do? I didn't borrow money for my business for at least five years. I started the company in 1998 on $90,000. One of my sisters had saved a great deal of money. She had $30,000 in the bank ten years ago and lent it to me. I was selling part of the company to pay the first five notes of the truck payment. The truck payment was $10,098 a month, every month. I had six months of reprieve when I got the truck so my sister gave me $30,000, and another friend gave me $27,000, and in return, they owned part of the stock in the company. A couple of other people put together $33,000 for me. With that $90,000 I had to get an office, buy a computer, buy furniture and pay my one employee.

I couldn't pay myself for six months, but I had a great 401(k). I have always been a great saver so my son and I lived off my 401(k) for about six months. Not one dime from the business came to me. The truck payments started six months after. At the time 90 percent of my business was Medicare, but Medicare would not approve one payment until they came out and reviewed the business. I had $90,000 to finance the company, and $10,000 of that went every month to pay for that truck.

Did I have a banker? A friend of mine who was in business with me had a relationship with Bank of America. In order for me to get the truck, this physician allowed me to use his bank account. He didn't put any money into the company, but he put his bank account up for me because he thought that this would be a good company. For that, I gave him a percentage of the company. I didn't know that I could go to a bank and borrow money. Those were lean times. I made my situation work, but I didn't take a salary. Had I taken a salary those years, perhaps the direction and the vision and where I am today would have been different.

It wasn't until 2002 that I bought my new Mercedes. That new car changed my entire life in terms of banking. When the financial officer said that my credit was good but I had too much "stuff" in my name, I realized that what he said was significant. I had been personally signing for all of the financial needs of this company. You have to do that as an entrepreneur early on. You don't have an option to say that the company is strong enough to stand alone. Obviously, I had great credit because every vehicle that we had I signed for personally. Eventually, I bought the Mercedes, but the loan officer said that I needed to talk to my banker about moving some of these assets out from underneath me personally, and putting them under the company.

Be Sure Your Bankers Pass the Test

Monday morning, I called my banker and had a meeting with her on Tuesday afternoon. At this point I had changed banks because I realized that I needed a bank that knew me. This particular bank had come in and practically wooed me, saying that they would do this and that—all of these great things for me and my money. I said "yes" to them. I thought this was my big opportunity because I didn't know that I could move assets from myself to the company.

I began talking to this banker whom I did not know. She was an African-American female and a vice president of that bank. She and her partner had come in and said, "We could do this and that for you. We will give you a lockbox." So all of my medical money went directly to this bank every day. It didn't even come to me because I had allowed them to set up a lockbox; all my patients' checks went directly to them every day. They had total control over it.

I was sitting in her big, beautiful office, telling her the story about trying to buy a new car, and how the salesman and the finance officer said that I needed to call my banker and move assets out from underneath me personally and put them under the company's name. As I began to explain what had happened, her first words to me were, "Girl—really?" I thought to myself, *We are not friends. You are my banker. All of my money comes to you and you say, "Girl— really?" This is business. Yes, we're both African-American females, but we don't socialize.* She failed the first test with me.

I tried another test, telling her that I needed a really good accountant. "Oh," she said, "I can help you with that." I said, "Okay," so she went to her Rolodex and started thumbing through a list of accountants. Her error was that she didn't just tell me the best one right off the top of her head. All I could think was, *I am your client! Give me the very best accountant that you have—and that's the one in your head, the one that you don't need to look up.* This was one of my first lessons in Banking 101. I just took all this in.

I finished our conversation that had now turned to "sister-girl." As my personal banker who had all of my money coming to her directly, she had made no business decisions for me at this point, nothing to help me. The disappointment was enormous because this wasn't even my bank. It too had come to me through a friend. They met with me because they knew someone else, a doctor friend of mine, and I had started to go with this bank because he was going to go there. I finished the "sister-girl" conversation, and by the time I got to the elevator I was calling back to my office with the one employee, Tracy. I told her, "You call every bank. I want to find four banks. I want a one-branch bank; no more than two and I want a small branch."

I Interview Banks—They Don't Interview Me

We called four banks. I took only banks that had one or two branches, no more, and I interviewed each one of those banks. I didn't allow the banks to interview me. The most important thing that you will get from this chapter is: Never allow a bank to interview you when it's your money going to the bank. I interviewed two banks, and I got very lucky with one of them. The president had been calling my office but never told me who he was. I went to meet him—I didn't know why he was calling. I learned that he had a personal relationship with my company. Someone in his family had been in my mobile unit and saw what I was doing.

The moment that I called that particular bank, the president already wanted to meet me because he knew the good work I was doing. I went to meet him, and that was the beginning of my Banking 101. I interviewed that president, but it had been to my advantage that he had been in my unit. He had seen what I was trying to bring to this area and was so excited that when I called to meet him, I ended up meeting the whole executive team. I didn't realize that I was putting enough money in that bank that I could expect to receive special privileges.

From that moment, I had a personal banker, someone to watch my account. If a check came in and needed to be moved to another account, my personal banker would do that. If I called the bank saying that I was on the road and needed anything, it was done. When I walked through that bank, from the teller all the way to the back, their attitude was, "Ms. Payne, how are you today?" I interviewed that bank. That was Banking 101.

Moving to an Entirely New Level

Then I went to level 201. That is where not only do the banks know you, but they can do things that you didn't know they could do. I continued to try to learn this process, that if banks know you and you provide them clean financials, a whole new world opens up. At this level, I learned that I had credit worthiness. The average Joe really doesn't get loans from the bank. The bank kept suggesting that I let them come pick up my deposits. They will come to you every day. You won't have to take your deposits to them. Some days we had thousands and thousands of dollars on the floor, patient checks, insurance checks and so forth. That was a problem. The bank said, "Let us take care of that." Every day they sent a courier to pick up the money because I didn't have time to go to the bank. This was significant. I had seen security couriers pick up money from restaurants and big corporations, but I didn't know that they came to little businesses like mine!

Then, if you are fortunate enough to reach a certain level of banking, you are assigned a personal financial banker. I have had a personal banker since 2002, and that personal banker manages all of my accounts. If you send a check to my bank and it doesn't look good or it doesn't make sense, my banker will call me. I never really went into the bank except when I needed to go personally because the banker always came to me. Initially, there was a fear factor involved with this because your banker can make or break your business life.

The next thing I learned is that you can outgrow your bank, and you have to know when you do. At one particular bank, the president decided that he would leave and start his own bank. The new bank was up north, fairly far from me. Once he left, the bank I was with wasn't moving to take care of his clients. They figured that at some point, his clients would leave. They didn't understand that I wasn't leaving because I couldn't go all the way to the new bank. I didn't have the time or the energy. I was still busy so as he left I knew that I either needed to go with him or find another bank. This is when I learned that when you get to a certain level, doors start to magically open. Every time I won a significant award, the first people to send me congratulations were banks. Bankers read the social pages. Every award that I won was significant and stated how much money I had made and how well I was doing.

I received flowers, gift certificates, bottles of wine and an invitation from each bank to come in and meet them. Banks began vying for my business. From this point, I switched banks to a larger bank. At any given time now, I have three to four banks that I work with. I have so many banking relationships that if one bank couldn't do what I needed, then the other one would. I learned never to allow just one person to handle all your money. Spread your wealth around! "Old money" banks don't always have the fortitude and the latitude to move forward. In moving to this new bank, I received loans to buy equipment, and once again, my banker came to see me. I never went to the bank. I had a personal banker again.

Know When It's Time to Go

How do I know when it's time to move to a new bank? If things change at the bank, if your banker changes and you have had a personal relationship with that banker, it's probably time to move. If you're just putting your money in the bank and no one knows who you are or is taking care of you, it's time to move.

When the bank no longer works for you, it's time to move. When that particular banker failed to give me the name of the very best accountant, she failed to give me an answer as to how to help me with my finances. Another change came about because my personal banker left; the relationship that I had with him no longer existed at that bank. Once he left, it was harder to do business. I had been assigned to a new banker who didn't know me. Once again, I was just putting my money into the bank without the bank going to work for me.

In 2004, we had grown so significantly that we needed to buy real estate because I was paying about $70,000 a year to rent someone else's space. This didn't make sense to me so I called my personal banker and said, "I want to buy a building because we are growing. We have enough money to put 20 percent down on whatever we buy." My banker came to the office for one of our meetings and said, "Colleen, every time I come in you're doing so many things that I'm having a hard time getting my arms around what you're doing."

I thought, *You've got to be kidding me. You are my personal banker and as I am growing you are growing with me. You are singing my praises, but now you tell me that it is getting hard to embrace what I'm doing!* He told me that the bank would help me buy a building but not a commercial property with tenants. He thought if he did that, he would be taking me away from what I was good at—medicine. He thought I might not be successful as a landlord of commercial tenants!

I knew I had started companies that were not "what I was good at." I had business relationships in areas that I "didn't know anything about," and here he was telling me I couldn't do some-

149

thing. As a result, I did the best thing that I knew to do: I called three banks and had three interviews. I had one at 8:00 A.M., one at 10:00 A.M. and one at 1:00 P.M. in my office. I decided that I wanted to buy a commercial property because that was what my business needed. Within seventy-two hours I had financing for a $3 million building. I had gone to another bank, and before I left that day, the banker said, "Great, it's done." My only question was, how could he 'get his arms around' what I was doing within just hours after meeting me, and my own banker couldn't? That was the sign to leave right there.

I was growing, and growing is a good thing in my case. I learned to have all of my financials in order when meeting with a new bank. Banking 101 has taught me that if my finances are in disarray, I will never get a dime. I can go back over every tax statement for every year that I have been in business. I have learned to keep my own books, and I can print off my own records. Having a banker who couldn't see my vision was the moment of decision for that bank relationship. It was over, and it was time to move on.

Your business can outgrow the people you work with relatively quickly, but you have to be able to know when that is. You have to be able to make a conscious decision that it is not personal, and it is time to leave.

I went out and secured another bank. Now, I have a personal relationship at all my banks. I have cell numbers, home numbers, and if I am out of town and I need money transferred, all it takes is a phone call or even just an e-mail. If something comes in on my account that doesn't look normal, my personal banker will call me. My banker comes to my office. When I am in the paper, I get a note from the president of the bank. My bank knows what's going on with me. I have found that you have to have your banker personally invested in you.

Your bank may have a number of good people working for it, but you know you have a good banker when you actually see your banker. I have a personal banker. I have a deposit express person. I can call my banker and say, "I need you to come and do this for me." He will be there in five minutes. That is the banker that you want. That is the banker that you need.

Why You Should Have More Than One Bank

There are times when a bank can't do certain things for you. That is why I always suggest having more than one bank. I always have four banks, and I know each banker. I know what they can and cannot do for me. I start another company every couple of years, so my banking relationships are vital. That's the sort of thing that you don't understand just starting out in your relationships with your bank. Because I need my banks on my side, part of my team, working for me, I change bankers and accountants often.

You can tell when a bank is going to work with you. This year, I decided that it was time to add a new bank, and there was a bank not too far from me. I called the bank and said, "This is who I am, this is who my company is and I need to open an account." They didn't know me from Adam—didn't know who or where I was. I gave them my information and within twenty-four hours, all of my bank papers were drawn up, my credit lines were drawn, personal and professional accounts were opened. Any paperwork that I have to do, the bank brings to me. I have learned to find banks that can work with me, that can see my vision and are looking out for my best financial interests.

Entrepreneur 101 Takeaway:

1. *Interview the bank. See how they are going to set your accounts up. Are you going to get a personal loan officer? How do they treat you at the bank? Are they going to make you work for the bank, or is the bank going to work for you?*

2. *Does the bank come to you? If the bank comes to you, then you have a good bank. Do you rank pulling the president of the company out of the bank? If you do, this is a bank that will serve you.*

3. *Have more than one bank working for you. One bank might be somewhat conservative in one area, and another might be too conservative in another. You need a team of banks that can fit your needs.*

4. *Move beyond the mind-set of, "I go to the bank and I put my money in it." The bank isn't just a place to keep your money. You want a relationship with your bank where you eventually are assigned a personal banker to watch your accounts for you and help maximize your money.*

5. *Finally, know your banker. Find out what services he or she is providing to you with your commercial account. Remember: Banking is about relationship, relationship, relationship!*

CHAPTER 21:

No Such Thing as Free Money

One of the biggest pitfalls for a new business owner is this idea that there is all of this "free money." People get the idea that there is money to start a business that you will never have to pay back. The truth of the matter is that there is no such thing as free money. Nobody in this country is going to give you money to start a business that you won't have to qualify for or pay back.

I have run into this mind-set, because I am an African-American woman, people think that I have received all sorts of financial incentives to start my business. You hear of the Economic Development office and the Small Business Administration office and many others. You get the impression that they're just waiting to give money to small business people. This isn't the case. They are not going to give you any money because there are guidelines that you have to meet, and one of them is that you have to be in business at least two years. How do you get that money? If the key is that you have to be in business for two years, then you need to have a business plan. These groups will tell you to write a business plan. You will spend a month of your life writing the best business plan imaginable because you are going to go and submit it to the agency. You will do all of this extra work trying to figure out how you can get all of this money. You'll get the impression that if you do everything that is required of you, then the money will pour in. This is not necessarily true.

If you have a business and you do receive money from one of these organizations, unless you are doing typical yard work or some other inconsequential business, you are not going to get enough money to last you. $20,000 or even $30,000 only puts you further in debt. Early on, I went to all of these meetings, trying to figure out where that free money was. What I saw was people getting paid to have you come in so they could keep their jobs.

Understand this: There is no free money. You will go to an office and they will play with you for months, leading you down this path believing that once you do this and once you do that, you'll get your money. You will keep coming in for weeks and months at a time, and they will make you do a business plan that doesn't make sense. You'll go back time and again, work yourself senseless, but there is no money. You'll do all this work, and those people will receive a check for sitting in the office. If you're lucky, you might eventually receive money. How does that help you? You will jump through hoops for weeks just for a few thousand dollars that may not be enough to help you.

Think about this. If there were free money out there, why would those people be in the office? They have heard all of the best ideas out there about various niche markets, but if there is free money, why haven't they taken the risk to become an entrepreneur? Why haven't they used that money themselves? Is it because they don't have the passion or desire? No, it's because no one is getting this so-called money. I asked a woman from one of these offices, "Who have you given any significant money to? I have so many people who come to my office to talk with me, but I have never seen anyone to whom you have given a significant amount of money. I know one woman you've given money to, and all you gave her was $20,000. She owns a publishing company. How long is that going to last her? And now she has to pay back that loan!"

So, Where Is All That Free Money?

If there really was free money, wouldn't it be free? No, when you start a business, understand once again that you need to do your research. Don't expect free money and don't expect someone to help you out when you are in a pinch. If your business starts to spiral, the money that they might give you will be like a band-aid on a broken leg. It is not going to help you. These government agencies rarely if ever give enough money to allow your business to survive. I have never seen anyone to whom they have given hundreds of thousands of dollars.

If you are a new entrepreneur, you don't have the two years of financials that are required. They don't tell you that until you get there. Then they come on strong about a business plan. All of this to demonstrate that they actually had somebody in their offices. How do I know? I did all of that, and recently I even went to Washington, D.C., with the Small Business Conference. When I was there, there seemed to be so many people who had received money to buy real estate. I called our local office back and told them that I would go out and buy more real estate if I knew that the government would subsidize it and I wouldn't have to come up with 20 percent down.

Don't Waste Your Time on Nothing

I was told I didn't qualify. Why not? Despite being a small business, I needed to be worth less than $1 million. How can your net worth be less than $1 million if you own a company and your company is successful? Their answer: "So many entrepreneurs and so many small business owners don't have your luck. They are not worth any money on paper." I questioned how I could have credit worthiness, a great business, but I couldn't receive any money because now I was worth too much. I asked for further information, but no one ever got back to me. What I realized is that the people in these agencies get paid based on seeing you, the entrepreneur. That is how they keep their jobs; they want you to come in. The more frequently you come in, the better. It looks as if they are actually helping someone.

Then there is the SBA. The SBA does have money to loan to some small businesses, and that is probably one of the better ways to go, but if you do visit them, they will go to your bank. If the bank funds the small business, the SBA will back the loan in case you default on it. Now, why would you have to go through a couple of months of filling out forms only to have the agencies find an SBA bank that will back your loan? Why not find the bank yourself that gives small business loans? These agencies will waste your time while they appear to be giving you hope for a loan. Why not cut out the agencies and go directly to a bank that participates with the SBA loan program?

Don't try to line up for the "free money"—it isn't there! Instead, create your own line of credit and make it a short one. Deal with one or two people. Remember, there is no "free line of credit." If you get a loan, you will have to pay the money back with interest. And if the people working in those offices hear all the great business ideas and have access to this "free money," why are they still working in that office? Why aren't they out starting new businesses? As an entrepreneur starting up, you can't get that money. If you have no financial reports, and you have no history, no one is going to just hand you money. Don't waste your time standing in the "free money" line—it doesn't exist.

The SBA is one of the only agencies that will help, but the SBA program doesn't actually loan any money. They just back your loan so in the event you default, then the lending agency has a guarantee that the SBA will repay the loan. You will fill out a mile of paperwork, but this program could possibly help your company. You'll have to have a few years in business, financials and a business plan. All the SBA will do is make it easier for the bank to give you that loan. Don't waste your time looking for the "free money." It doesn't exist!

Entrepreneur 101 Takeaway:

There is no such thing as free money—no such thing as a start-up loan you won't have to pay back. Save yourself the headache of filling out paperwork for months on end only to receive a few thousand dollars. Use that time and effort to find real financing to start your business.

CHAPTER 22:

Building Your Team

It is rare when you start a business that you will have the financial ability to bring together all the professionals you need in-house in your building. The team of outside professionals you create is a #1 priority. Who needs to be on your team? First, you have to have a great attorney—not just a good attorney, and that's who most of us start out with—but a great attorney who will always be available to you, who can get you out of any situation and who will provide sound legal advice at any moment. Just like your banker, your attorney needs to know you personally.

Second, having a great relationship with the banker is significant to your success. I can't stress that strongly enough. Finally, you will need a financial counselor, an accountant/CPA. If you don't have clean financials, if you don't know where your money is, how you got it and what is happening to it, you will never grow. The three most important people on your team are those three: your attorney, your banker and your accountant.

The need for an attorney speaks for itself. Just being in business, you will need an attorney. I have been very fortunate, and I have never been sued, but MCI writes a large number of contracts.

My attorney writes a really good contract. He has been with me almost since day one. He has moved his office and I have moved with him because I know that whenever he writes a contract for me, it's an excellent one. I am a small company, and I have had to fight huge corporations and won because they underestimated the value of my attorney. He is the one member of my professional staff that I have kept because no matter what, my attorney knows me, and he is going to work his hardest to get me out of any situation. Sometimes we clash, but he has been a valuable part of my team.

My accountants have been like my bankers. Sometimes throughout the process, you grow beyond people and have to move on. I started with a small accountant, and this company grew beyond what he could do for me. I think that historically I have changed accountants just about every two years. Have those been hard changes? Yes, but it is just the same situation as your banker. You have to know when to go. I had to learn early on that not knowing anything about the financial world, the business world and owning a company could hurt me. I had to work really hard because I had to know where my money was and what I was doing.

Know the Jobs Your Team Members Perform

My first accountant really caused me heartache. I didn't know anything about paying employee tax. He simply calculated my employee tax and left the records in his office. He seemed to think that one day I would show up and pay them. I didn't know that he wasn't paying employee tax on my behalf. I wound up with a $100,000 lesson when the I.R.S. notified me that I had not paid those taxes and they started putting tax holds on my bank accounts. I had already switched over to a payroll company, but the accountant never told me about paying the payroll taxes. Once this happened, I bought a program to run and manage my internal finances.

Since that time, I have never ever allowed anyone else to sign off for me. I have never allowed anyone to keep books outside my company where I couldn't see them. I spent every waking day learning my financial software. I practiced with my own money, and I put my own bills in to learn how to manage it. I had to learn this lesson the hard way after putting my trust in someone else's expertise.

Over the last ten years, people have asked me how I learned to manage my business finances. I tell them that I had to learn how to do them. I had to understand my business finances because if I didn't know what my accountant was doing, there was no way I could know if he was doing it correctly or not. Part of my success has come from the fact that I understand every job. I may not be able to do it myself, but I can tell if it's being done correctly or not. I'm very hands-on, and this is the best way I can keep on top of my own business. I think my success speaks for itself.

How do you go about hiring a good accountant so you can avoid my expensive lesson or others like it? Hire someone who is willing to come to you at least once a month early on in your professional relationship. Never give anyone the authorization to sign your name for you. Finally, know your own finances—I don't think anyone can be successful who doesn't. Find a software program that makes sense to you. Learn that program, and take care to operate your company from within. I am not opposed to doing it another way, but this is what worked for me.

When my accountant came on board, I listed all of my equipment. I can tell you what my net worth is. I don't have to call him on the phone. I can tell you what my accounts payable are. It is so important that you know your own finances. Don't take for granted that people are going to do right by you all of the time because they won't. Anytime you pay someone to work, you are paying that person to eat and you want him to do a good job for you. If you don't thoroughly understand your finances, you will have no idea if he is doing a good or a bad job for you.

Do It Until You Know What It's About

One of the things that I didn't understand was payroll. After my incident with the payroll tax, I actually started doing my own payroll in-house. This isn't a good idea at all, but I did it because that was the one thing that caused me a problem, and the one thing I didn't understand. I did payroll for a year. That way, never again would anyone ever cause me a problem with my payroll. When I find a hole or a weakness, I learn everything I can so that the problem will never occur again.

I'm the captain of the ship that is my company. I may not know exactly how to put up the sails, but I can tell when it has been done correctly or not! This kind of knowledge involves doing my homework—a lot of it. Too many people don't put in the time and energy to learn accounting or a program to run their company because they say that this is not what they are good at. You don't have to be good at everything. All that you have to do is have an understanding of the procedure. I can't do my taxes, but I do know if my accountant has made a mistake, I understand when he didn't do something correctly and I understand when he has facilitated something that doesn't make sense.

If you don't understand your money when you start a business, how are you going to understand it when you get bigger? You can wind up having people manage so much of your life that you don't know when they are making serious mistakes that can cause you great trouble. I decided I was going to know my business from the bottom up, and many times I had to do it the hard way. I don't know whether or not I would repeat some of the practices I used early on—probably not—but I think that I definitely would repeat knowing exactly where my money is. Today, the reason that my banks work so well with me is if they call me for a financial or a profit and loss statement, I can print my own. I want my financial statements that work with my software to work with my accountants.

Before I made these decisions to know my business, I had no financial records in-house. I had nothing. I didn't have a program. I couldn't look at anything. I don't even know that I could have written a check in-house on the program we had. After I decided to know my own financials, I spent every waking moment of every day putting all of my information into that software. I didn't know what I was doing, but I learned because I decided never again would I be caught in a bad situation. Even now, the reason I change accountants so often is that if I catch your errors [I'm not an accountant] and if I am able to see your mistakes, then are you really capable of performing my financial work? As a professional you should review your work before presenting it to your client. If I continuously see your errors, then it's no longer a viable working relationship. That is why I am willing to change accountants so frequently, because sometimes professionals stop working for you, the client. You have to be willing to make changes. It's just business.

It's Not Personal—It's Business

Many of the people that I have had in my professional life have been my friends because I want you to be my friend if you are working with my money or if you are my banker. I am interested in you, and I am interested in how you live and all of those things, but when you start making mistakes, I remember that it is always business, nothing personal. I am not saying that at the first mistake it's time to go, but the second or third mistakes? Are the mistakes costly and I can see them? If so, then, yes, it is 100 percent time to go. You have to be a strong person to do that with people that you have established relationships with. It is always business, what's good for the company, and nothing personal. It is another one of those Catch 22's—how involved do you want to be in your company? How much are you willing to make those hard decisions about who goes? The answer is another question: How successful do you want to be?

There is another member of the team who has to be on top of things: you. You have got to know what needs to happen in your business; many people don't want to expend the time and energy to do that. They have a great idea, and they're like an artist. Sometimes an artist is skilled in their art, but terrible when it comes to the business side of their work. I told a good friend of mine that you have to be able to merge the two sides—your "art" and your "business." I am really good at medicine, but I have become better at business. I have to know which hat to wear and when to wear it. I try to wear a mixture of both every day. I may be wearing ten hats a day, but I make sure that I am wearing both my medicine and my business hats every day. I am doing what makes good medical sense *and* what makes good business sense.

You are the leader of your business. The great leader knows what has to be done and when; you may not be the one doing it because you can't do everything. If you could, you wouldn't need to hire an attorney or an accountant or a banker. You would *be* the accountant or the attorney or the banker. Instead, you need to be able to tell when they are doing what they are supposed to be doing. This requires responsibility and a commitment to self-education on your part. Those are the parts that we entrepreneurs sometimes want to cut short. We want to do our business, but to me, doing your business means knowing all aspects of it so that you can do it with excellence. You have to know the business side as well as your area of professional expertise.

I have talked with people who have told me that they outsource all of their legal and financial work. Even if you can do that, you still have to know that there are times you need to know what is going on with your business. It is not enough to know the creative end of the business; you need to know the *business* end of your business, too. Sometimes when we are doing great in business but we don't know what has transpired to get us there, we won't understand what is necessary to *keep* us there. No matter how well your business is running, no matter how advanced you are as an entrepreneur, you will need to be able to look at your business as a whole and say, "I know how this process works. I know when it's working correctly, and I can tell when it isn't." The ideal is for your company to grow to the point where you can't do all of the day-to-day operations yourself. However, if you have grown up with your business and learned the day-to-day operations, you can tell if something doesn't make sense. Even though I wouldn't dare go out and do my attorney's work, I can help him achieve what he needs for my company. Am I going to help my accountant? My banker? Absolutely! To do that, I need to stay on top of the game myself.

Entrepreneur Takeaway 101:

Do the homework—the hard work—necessary to understand every function and process you hire a team to do. Be willing to make changes when you find that your team isn't doing its job, or when you outgrow your team. Remember: It's business and not personal.

CHAPTER 23:

Merging the Two: You and Your Company

We have already touched on merging you and the company. Merging you and your company allows you to brand yourself and your company. Yet there is a time where you and the company need to go on separate paths as well. In the beginning, the two of you have to be merged because of banking. When you first start up, the company cannot buy anything. When you are trying to buy a $1 million piece of equipment, the company doesn't have the longevity to stand alone. You need to be the co-signer or author of that bank loan. You and your business almost become one single credit report.

When I first started MCI, I used to look at my credit report and think of what MCI could do; now I can look at it and only see me. Today, the company and I each have our own report. But in those early years, merging the two of us was of major significance.

Initially, that merging is absolutely necessary. The credit worthiness of your company and how the two of you look on paper is great. All of a sudden, however, you realize that merging the two of you has now made you one entity. You have to figure out how to "unmerge" you. Why? If something were to happen to you and you and the company are inseparable, once you're no longer around, the company no longer exists, and neither do its contacts and relationships

Sell It Before I'm in the Ground

About five years ago, I was talking with my husband and I asked that if, God forbid, something were to happen to me, what would he do with the company? Realizing that the company and I are completely merged with each other, I told him to sell this company before I am even in the ground because once I am gone, it wouldn't be worth much of anything.

People doing business with MCI were actually doing business with me. If I were gone, there would be no company to do business with. This realization caused me to change my priorities. From that moment, I was determined to separate myself from MCI.

This merging and unmerging relationship between you and your company is very much like the relationship of a parent to a child. When a baby is born, it is helpless. The mother needs to merge its needs with hers. She needs to spend all her time with that baby or it won't survive. In the beginning years of your company, it's imperative to merge yourself with the company. Your reputation, your awards, your persona help brand the company for success. In the beginning, your credit rating is the company's credit rating because the company doesn't have one yet. The survival of your company in the early years depends on you merging yourself with it.

However, if you don't separate yourself to some degree from the company, instead of that relationship being positive, it turns negative. Instead of helping the company survive, the merged relationship begins to threaten the company's survival. When I first had my son, I couldn't think of him as a completely separate being from me because he could not have survived on his own. However, he is now growing up into a young man, and if his mother doesn't help him become a "stand alone" being, he will never be able to survive by himself.

Can Your Business Survive on Its Own?

It was a shock to me to realize that the company could not survive on its own, because we were much too identified. All of the contracts that came in were from people who knew me personally. All of the doctors who worked with us knew me personally. I have spent the last few years of this company separating the two of us because we reached a fork in the road where one of us had to turn right and one of us had to turn left. I have spent the better part of the last few years not having many people know that I owned the company.

I was riding with a doctor many years ago and he asked me why I didn't tell people that I owned MCI. I told him that this company had to stand on its own. If I continued to scream from the mountaintops that I owned it, then people would treat the company a certain way, do business with it only because of me. Instead, doctors need to be able to send their patients here and do business with us not because one individual is sitting at the helm, but because we do a really good job.

I still bring a lot of attention to MCI, but people often don't put it together that I actually own it—and that is fine with me. It was just this year—ten years into operation—that I finally got a business card saying President/Owner. My card always has been Director of Operations because I do not want to be the face of this company. MCI needs to survive. We have people who work here whose livelihood depends on this company thriving. I never want to see my staff out of work just because something has happened to me.

Do I think that someday I very well may say, "This has been great! I have had my fun running this company. It's been my passion—but now it's time for me to quit"? Yes, I do. But if I don't separate myself from MCI, what will happen to my employees? And what will happen to the hospitals, doctors and patients we serve? I have a responsibility that if something were ever to happen to me or if this company were sold, my employees would still have a job. Part of my business ethics concerns their future. And part of those same ethics is concerned with our clients. This is a valuable service we provide for them, and I believe in it. I have passion for it. It is such a necessary service that people deserve to be able to have it even if I am gone.

Unmerge to Protect the Business— and the People Who Need It

I believe that MCI is much bigger than I am, much bigger than my personal life and desires. It doesn't really have that much to do with me anymore. MCI is a business. My staff still has to have jobs so they can maintain. Our patients need the care we provide. I just get to sit in the big office. I enjoy coming to work so I come every day. I don't have to do that. No one makes me come every day, but I do it because I love this work. And yet, I have spent four years untangling myself from this company. It should be able to go on without me, almost on autopilot.

Do I want to do this the rest of my life? I started this company when I was thirty-three and always said that at forty-five, I wanted to retire. Just a few more months, and I can begin to look at ways to do that. At some point this company will grow outside of where I am comfortable. Have I received every possible award that I could? No, but I'm very close to it. This company still remains a passion and a joy for me, but there is more to me than MCI—it's not the sum total of my life. I have accomplished so much for a girl from Spencer, Oklahoma. What else could I do? I will have to start another chapter in my life, find another mountain to climb. When I go on to that next chapter, I am determined that MCI will survive. I am "unmerging" the company I merged myself with to ensure its future and that of its employees and the clients we serve.

Entrepreneur 101 Takeaway:

In the early years of your company, you have to merge yourself with it to ensure its survival. As time progresses, you will have to draw the line between yourself and the company so it can survive without you.

CHAPTER 24:

Marketing to People Classes

I began as a technologist. I was educated, but I certainly wasn't at the same level with people who had the power to provide us multimillion dollar contracts. I wasn't in the right arena to start talking to hospital administrators; up to that point, I had been a worker bee. It is very difficult to make that transition from worker bee to administrator, handling business and trying to sit in a corporate boardroom. I had to learn to market myself and MCI to people of all different socioeconomic classes. That involved presenting our business to wealthy and powerful executives and to people much further down the chain from where I was. It involved crossing ethnic lines to market to people from different backgrounds.

Like most aspects of being an entrepreneur, making the transition from worker bee tech to company owner was a journey. At first, I found myself doing more of the listening while people talked to me. Inside, I was trying to be composed, sitting correctly, ready with a vocabulary that demonstrated my knowledge and expertise—it wasn't just about the business itself. From the moment you walk in, people begin assessing you as to how you are dressed, whether or not you look like you are in business and whether or not you look like you can stay in business. To deal with different classes of people, you really have to come into your own in learning how to talk to people without being intimidated

Intimidated at First

I don't think you can start a small business and immediately be on the same level as some of the people with whom you are going to do business. Is it an eventual possibility? Yes, it is, and I think achieving that ability to talk on an equal level is a work in progress in terms of understanding that those boundaries and social classes exist, and determining that you are going to transcend those in your business life.

One thing I realized early on was that I was more educated in nuclear medicine than the people with whom I was going to meet. When I walked into that room, I knew I was selling a product, and I understood that product better than anyone else there. I knew why I was there and what I needed to sell. That in itself gave me an edge. No matter what questions people threw at me, if it was about nuclear medicine, then I was all right. I was the most educated person in the room on that subject. It didn't matter who was there, what they made, what they drove, what kind of house they lived in. I was a very good nuclear medicine technologist. I was at the top of my game, and that helped me navigate the distance across the socioeconomic divide. I knew I was there to get the contract.

There was another aspect of crossing these boundaries. I still needed to be personable, I needed to share details about my life and work because everyone wants "intro talk." In fact, that intro talk is highly important. If your intro talk is not smooth, people don't tend to hear anything else you have to say. That may be one reason that when you go into a meeting, the first thing people talk about is the weather. In Tulsa, Oklahoma, where our seasons can change from day to day, if not hour to hour, the weather is an easy icebreaker. You can never go wrong talking about the weather, how hot it is or how cold it's getting. Everyone can sound intelligent at that level.

When you move outside your socioeconomic level, keep it simple. If I'm talking to professional golfers, I don't talk about golf, because I don't play the sport. Stick to what you know and keep the small talk very nominal to get started. Then, as the success of your company grows and you have more exposure to people of all venues, you can begin to branch out.

Remember, this is just a level of transition that you are going through, and it may be uncomfortable at first. Know your product and master the intro conversation. People will be convinced that you are intelligent and capable. I stuck with the weather for a long time even because I knew that I was out of my social class. People don't talk about the social classes in the U.S., but we absolutely 100 percent know our class. My secret confidence-booster was the knowledge that I was the expert on nuclear medicine in the room.

Hone Your Intro Talk

At other times, my intro talk will consist of volume statistics for the hospital. We have more injuries in the summer, specifically injuries to children, because people are outdoors more. In the summer, my intro talk may concern peak times that clinics are full. When I am talking to people concerned with health care, these commonalities make sense. My intro talk is important because people sum you up in the first five to ten minutes. That is the moment when you need to have something to say that indicates your intelligence and understanding, so I use statistics concerning clinics in the warm weather, and then I'm back to ice and snow in the winter. You can't really win somebody back after that first impression, so your first moments of conversation are the most important because it is that determining factor that either gets you to the next level or doesn't.

Talking isn't the only way that you can make that vital first impression. Listening is important. First, if you have listened in different meetings, you have picked up the kind of small talk that is part of that particular area. Listening is a very important aspect of crossing those social barriers. I tend to take in what you're saying so I can digest it later. It is like reading an e-mail. I can go back and read your e-mail, if it is a significant one, two or three times because I want to hear what you're not saying in words. You always want to listen. I've seen an evolution in being able to talk to different classes of people. I have learned to project the idea that I'm comfortable in this conversation. It is all about attitude and perception.

Be Ready to Adjust Either Direction

You can learn to step up or down in the social arena. You have to do both. Sometimes I go to offices to where the woman at the desk makes maybe $10 an hour, but I have to talk to her so she feels drawn into my conversation. I don't want to raise a barrier of defensiveness in her by making her feel that I am "superior." Inside, I remind myself that while my jewelry might be a little better, my clothes might be a little more expensive, we do the same job. You're not trying to be a phony or sell yourself out; you are just not explaining the whole you. If you walk in the middle, you can adjust up or down, but you have to be able to adjust. How do you do that? My tool is my projection that you and I are pretty much in the same arena. This is important—that woman may be the person you really need to speak to, or she might be the gate-keeper to the physician.

I try to keep the playing field level. The business card I use most often says Director of Operations. It implies that I work for MCI. As a director, I can adjust in either direction, but as a president and owner I can never adjust down. And once again, listening is important because it allows me judge as to which direction I need to adjust.

Entrepreneur 101 Takeaway:

Developing the attitude that you can talk to anyone about your business because you are rock-solid in your knowledge of it involves several components. They include:

1. **Self esteem.** If you walk in knowing that you're worth a million bucks, then you are worth a million bucks.

2. **Projection.** The way you appear, your clothes and grooming, projects that you deserve to be where you are.

3. **How you speak.** You are being interviewed for that contract. Hone your interview skills.

4. ***Know why you are there.*** *Remember, you are the expert in your field in that meeting. I used to remind myself that I was smarter than everyone in the room when it came to nuclear medicine. I may not have been the smartest person in the room, but I walked into the room with a level of confidence that came from my knowledge of my field.*

CHAPTER 25:

No Press Like
Free Press

I think this is the best "entrepreneur's read-me chapter" because whoever said there is no press like free press certainly knew what she was talking about. You can place an ad in any paper, people will see the ad—but will it make you stand out? If you are one of the big competitors—Coke, Nike—your ad will definitely set you apart. However, as a small entrepreneur, you don't have the budget to do a million dollar commercial that will instantly brand you and your company. How can you get press without paying for it and make it work for you?

Praise from Others Is Priceless

The one best way to get press is to get recognized for something incredible that you have done. People will read a human interest story even while they ignore advertising. Your story will be picked up by the wire, the newspapers and the television stations. That press, having one article picked up by your local TV stations, will be worth $20,000 to $30,000. And it's free. I came up with a great idea about six years ago, shortly after I started this company. I didn't have a huge marketing budget. How could I call attention to MCI? I can't give myself 100 percent credit for this idea because my sister helped me. She and I decided to submit my name for Business Innovator of the Year. I was providing a good community service, but no one knew who I was. I was taking this mobile truck to all of the rural areas in Oklahoma to provide nuclear medicine to people who couldn't easily reach the urban areas. I was helping staff the hospitals, but I was doing it all under the radar because I was a worker bee. How could I get recognized as a good businesswoman, and not for that alone, but for being a woman business owner whose company was doing good work?

Right around December of 2002, my sister and I read that *Black Enterprise* magazine was giving this award. She decided to submit an application. There was no way in Oklahoma that I would win, but we decided to do it anyway. My sister nominated me, and we worked all weekend to create my submissions binder before the deadline a few days away. I didn't think too much about it—after all, I was in Oklahoma.

In March, we received a notice from *Black Enterprise* that I was one of the finalists who had been chosen from around the country. The magazine notified me that I was invited to attend the award ceremony. I went not knowing whether or not I had won—it was that top secret. The award ceremony was held in Nashville, Tennessee, during a huge gala and three-day conference. I won that award, and it set me on the path of great success. I had an opportunity to speak with Mr. Earl Graves of *Black Enterprise,* thanking him that my business won—all the way from Oklahoma.

This award started me on the path of free press when I got back to Oklahoma. The entire state was happy to know that I had won Business Innovator of the Year for the entire nation for *Black Enterprise*. The *Tulsa World* ran a full-page article in the business section about my company. "Her heart is in it," it states in the title. From that article alone came a million dollar contract that just landed in my lap. Shortly after that, we were in negotiations with a multimillion dollar corporation doing business all across Oklahoma. Shortly after that article came out in the paper, I happened to have my meeting with this corporation. I walked into the director's office, and the first thing he mentioned was my winning that award. "We'd love to work with you!" Winning that award gave me great credibility. I could never have bought the recognition that it gave me and MCI. That was free press way beyond anything I could have imagined.

Stop Paying for Ads That People Forget

What makes free press so valuable is that you aren't paying someone to say what you want them to say. When you receive free press, the media are saying whatever needs to be said about you. If it's good—and this was—it boosts your credibility because someone from the outside is praising you and holding you up to the public. I rarely ever buy advertising now.

After that article, I made it my goal to win every award possible. One of the next major awards that I won was the Pinnacle award from the Mayor's Commission on the Status of Women. Once more, the result was incredible press for Mobile Cardiac Imaging and MCI Diagnostic Center. Once more, this was someone else saying that we were doing a quality job, that we were an outstanding company. I wasn't saying it—the people who mattered most were saying it!

When a peer group who has clout and status praises your work, you receive credibility that is not only well-deserved but is impossible to purchase through ads. Submitting my application binders—sometimes over a hundred pages, complete with financial information—has required time and effort, but it has more than paid off in the free press and attention drawn to my business.

In 2006, I was Small Business Person for Tulsa, and in 2007 Small Business Person for the entire state of Oklahoma. In 2006, we were named one of the 5,000 fastest-growing companies by INC 500. Any press you receive—whether it's for you or for the company—gives you the best, positive image you can have.

It doesn't matter what you are involved in; someone has an award out there for you—for the best lawn mower repairman or the best schoolteacher. Everyone wants to know, "Who is doing the very best?" Each award wins you the free recognition you need to promote your business to its highest potential.

Awards and More

My avenue to free press was that of accolades, awards and recognition for my company for bringing something into this community that hadn't been done before. People will remember seeing you on TV or recall reading an article in the paper far more than they will remember that expensive ad. But my road to free press isn't the only one. There are numerous ways to garner the attention your business deserves.

You can give back to your community through community investment in student scholarships, and by just being a part of the community. You can volunteer your time or adopt a family. Some of those won't give you recognition, but done sincerely, they will pave the way for you to sit on various boards and have your company recognized. I am not a huge fan of giving away all of your time—I think that the more boards you sit on, the less time you have to do your actual job. However, giving back to your community by volunteering your employees is good for the community, for your employees and for your business. Great employees can do great things, and I encourage my employees to volunteer. It's just good to do, and the free press is an added benefit.

You have to go down the road that makes sense for you. What made sense for me were the awards. I didn't have a budget for spending $5,000 or $10,000 a month on marketing. The awards were my best marketing tool. My company has the best public relations team: me. I used what we had consistently, and it has caused us to do well in the marketing arena. Once again, free press connects to the idea of branding yourself, setting yourself apart. Find the arena that fits your personality, that is authentic for you as an entrepreneur. And remember, there's no press like free press!

Entrepreneur 101 Takeaway:

Find the area that fits with your personality that will lead to free press. One award, one article or TV spot highlighting your employees volunteering will bring you the kind of positive attention that puts a seal of approval on your company. The credibility it will bring to your business equals thousands, if not millions, in new business.

CHAPTER 26:

Awards and Accolades Can Mean a Million Dollars

When I look at the awards on my walls, I can still see every ceremony. I can remember just about every outfit that I wore because those awards are so significant, not just to me but in the journey of my company's success. I take it all a step further in making those awards on the wall mean more than just metal and wood. I have signatures on my e-mail, for example, that lets you know who I am: Colleen J. Payne-Nabors, 2007 Oklahoma Small Business Person of the Year. I sign everything with that because it is a short-lived award—but can have lasting benefits. I capitalized on it while I had it.

When our company sends out a fax, it will say "Small Business Company of the Year," or "Pinnacle Award Winner" or "GE Award for Excellence." You'll see every award that I or my company have ever won over and over. Every month we change them so you see all of the different awards. Making those awards work for you is not just about taking those plaques and sticking them on your wall. It's making sure that people know you're successful. People want to know that other people think you are successful. It's like receiving a clean bill of health because somebody else has deemed you worthy. You have received someone's stamp of approval.

One item we have not modified or changed very much is the company logo because I like consistency, and I don't think that you play around with your logo. You can add to it, however, and I do have a special logo heading that says Small Business Person of the Year. We rotate every award we have won through our business paperwork, such as our faxes. We have so many that we can change them out every month. Over that month, it's firmly ingrained in you that we were in Chicago or that I met Bill Clinton, for example. Initially, I had won so many awards that I thought I shouldn't try for any more. I changed my mind, because I realized that continuing to win builds credibility, mine and MCI's. It says, "I did it before, and I'm doing it now!" Those awards are significant, but you have to make them work for you. Almost every award will come with some type of press release or some type of acknowledgment—you can choose how to use it to your best advantage.

Awards are proof that you are doing good work, and it all goes back into keeping your brand clean and safe and protecting it just like you would a child. It's one thing to have an award or two, but if you have a whole wall full, it's like saying that you are receiving unqualified approval, and your quality has been solidly proven over a period of time. People don't even know that I own the company; the recognition goes to MCI Diagnostic Center. MCI is the primary reason I went after these awards. I wanted my company to receive the press it so deserved.

I am in a competitive industry, and no other competitor in my area by far has won as many awards as MCI and I have. I look on the wall in my office and realize that those aren't just pieces of paper. Those awards aren't just photos, metal and wood. They aren't just beautifully etched pieces of glass, and they're not just a moment of glory for Colleen Payne-Nabors. They are each a paving stone in the road to success, and that success is for MCI. It's not about me. I never lose track of what these awards are really about. They are about the recognition of my company, making my company the focal point of everything I do. Yes, I get to dress up, walk across the stage and receive that award, but I represent Mobile Cardiac Imagining, MCI Diagnostic Center. They are the reason I win.

Entrepreneur 101 Takeaway:

Put those accolades and awards to work by finding creative ways to keep them before the public and your customers. Tagged along the bottom of an e-mail, printed on the faxes and billing, you prolong the momentum of the excitement and attention that your business receives each time you win an award. Don't let them just sit on the wall or on a table—get them busy promoting your company.

CHAPTER 27:

The Title Next to Your Name

The title next to your name is probably the most important aspect of all you are doing when you are establishing your company. What title do you choose? Does it have to be the "biggest" title in the company? Do you have to scream to the world that this is your company? Is that the first thing people need to know about you when they meet you?

You lose a great deal by announcing that you are the owner in that "title next to your name." When I started my company, my title was and remains Director of Operations. I chose this title strategically because it allows me to "climb" up or down when I go out to meet people. I can choose to reveal that I am not only Director of Operations, but I am also Founder, Owner and President if I feel I need to.

I have learned, however, that there is information I need to get from you, and depending on what level I appear to be on—and who I'm talking to—I may not get that information. If you are having a problem or something didn't get done, and you realize that you are talking to the owner of MCI, I have found that I may not get all the information I need. People aren't always completely truthful when they realize they are talking to the owner of the company; they don't want to hurt your feelings if your company has done something wrong. They will make their complaint to someone else who will pass it along to the person in charge rather than tell the owner or president directly.

Don't Tell All Your Business

As Director of Operations, I can move in and out of being owner or president. In fact, I've done this for many years—sometimes revealing that I own MCI, and sometimes not. It's not that I'm hiding who I am, but I have learned that you don't necessarily have to tell all your business. If I am the Director of Operations, you are more likely to tell me that you didn't get that report back. At that point, I can go into owner mode, getting on the phone to get it done for you. When clients view me as Director of Operations, I can see discrepancies in our service and find out what isn't being done that should be. However, if my card says President, clients are less likely to level with me. If you believe that I am a working person, laboring in the trenches, employed by someone else, I am likely to get more information from you. Your attitude will probably be, "Look, I know you don't own the company, but here is what is going on. This is my problem." You feel comfortable being absolutely honest with me.

This goes back to what I have said about the different socioeconomic classes. If I am talking to the office manager, that person is probably making a good salary. Maybe I'm making a higher salary, but that manager won't be aware of it. All he/she will know is that I'm the Director of Operations. That creates an automatic level of comfort. They are not talking to someone far above them, but to someone in a similar situation. The manager is likely to give me information that he might not automatically tell someone else—particularly if that "someone else" is the owner whom he perceives as being far above him on the socioeconomic scale.

Using the title of Director of Operations worked to my advantage for many years. I could talk to you one-on-one, and you would feel free to tell me everything that I needed to know—honest feedback as to whether or not we were doing a good job. When you have President/Owner in your title, you create a barrier that prevents people from speaking candidly to you. If clients perceive that they are on a different socioeconomic plane than you are, they will be hesitant in telling you what's wrong. They just want the problem fixed, but they don't want to take your business. If you are perceived as being like them, just working for "the man" yourself, they are likely to open up as to what the situation really is.

I encourage people to consider what title they put on their business card. It has only been in the last year that I even got another business card that said President/CEO. I have always known who I am. I know who I am when I go home and put my feet up at night after working myself bone tired. What title I carry doesn't mean that much to me, but titles are significant. For example, when my administrator and I meet clients, she goes by the title of Administrator, and I am the Director of Operations. Which one of us are they going to talk to? They will talk to her, and I can observe what they are saying. I can look at her and say "yes" or "no." They have no idea on what basis I am saying "yes" or "no" because I am perceived as the Operations Director. Working this way gives me insight into my company.

Choose a Title with Flexibility

Having a title like Director of Operations also gives me tremendous flexibility. Many years ago, I was riding with a doctor who is a good friend of mine. He asked, "Colleen, if I owned this company, I would be screaming it from the rooftops, just telling everyone. Why is it that you don't tell anyone and your card says Director of Operations?" I replied that I had chosen to do this my way because I was in a nontraditional environment, in a science modality where women are not generally expected to excel. I was driving a truck, typically a male-dominated arena, and on top of it, I was also an African-American woman. I didn't have to identify who I was to do a good job with my business, although early on when I first started the business, people could not perceive that a technologist making $50,000 a year could buy a $654,000 truck.

If I mentioned that I owned the company, people couldn't grasp that. To them, I was just the "front man." I found that people's disbelief that I could own the company actually started to work in my favor. When no one thought I was the business owner, I had more freedom to do a great job and convince them that we were an excellent company. It took all the pressure off of me of trying to "be the owner" and convince them that we really could do a good job.

The title next to your name needs to be well thought out. Consider the business arena that you are in, the type of business that you do and think about having two sets of business cards, one of which tells what you actually do to get paid. If you're an entrepreneur just starting out, trust me—you will be wearing at least ten hats. Pick a job that will allow you to relate to the ordinary person who is sending business to your company. Then, be able to switch those hats and say, "Okay, I am actually the president," which will allow you access to certain people higher up. Pick a title that best suits you for the situation.

I have always led this company as Director of Operations, but at any given moment I can step aside and become the president and owner. However, with the Director of Operations title, people just assume that I am highly informed about this company, I know every aspect of it and I could even give them a decision on the spot. The flexibility in my title lets me make those decisions without having to call back to the office, and yet I didn't tip my hand that I was the owner.

Tell Your Ego to Take a Rest

What do you lose if your ego gets in the way and you just have to put the top title next to your name? You lose that "common man" approach. You can miss valuable information. The gatekeepers at the client's office, such as the receptionists, will tell me exactly how we are doing if I am just the Director of Operations, but all of that goes away if she thinks I am the owner of MCI. That flexible title lets me live in both worlds—the world where I get the straight story from the people in the trenches, and the world where I can talk with CEOs and corporation presidents on the same level.

Another way a flexible title benefitted me was starting a business as a woman, an African-American woman in a medical field—I didn't fit the normal expectations. Having a title like Director of Operations suggested that someone else was president, that I operated under someone else's authority, that there was someone else behind me calling the shots. It's not fair, it's not right, but that title gave the impression that a man ran MCI—and that gave my company more clout as a larger organization. If I tried to tell people—especially a group of men—that I owned MCI, no one believed me.

Many years ago, when I first started the company, I was invited to meet with one of the biggest cardiology groups in Tulsa. They summoned me to their office, and I was extremely excited thinking that I had made it and they were going to use my services. Life was going to be great; all my hard work had paid off. I came dressed as owner of MCI, ready with my small talk, and anticipating that when I left, I'd be holding one of the biggest contracts imaginable.

It was an intimidating group of six doctors and the CEO/Administrator of this cardiology group. They only had one question: "Who owns the company?" I sank about five inches in my chair, but I didn't let on. I realized that I wasn't there to sign a contract. When I told them that I owned MCI, they didn't believe me. They just couldn't believe that an African-American woman owned MCI. That I had come in and taken their contracts from them because I was competing with this group. They were convinced that there had to be someone behind me, that I couldn't have started this company. They just wanted to know who was "behind me" at MCI.

I realized at that point, probably about a year after I started the business, that it wasn't important for me to tell who owned the company. No one seemed to believe that I did. That has carried over to today. I opened another clinic several years ago, and one of the doctors approached one of my employees and asked who owned us. Almost ten years later, people still can't believe that this business could be operated by a nonphysician. For years after that conversation, I just said that the company is privately held. Ninety percent of the time it made sense and worked for everyone. If you pressed me, I would tell you that I owned the company. Even now, people come to speak to the owner of the company and are surprised when an African-American woman walks around the corner.

Doing What's Best for Your Business

I have chosen to put Director of Operations on my card for the betterment of MCI. I have found that calling myself Owner/President causes me to miss the common man or woman. I rarely get their opinions if they perceive me as the owner of MCI. The information they have is priceless. Their opinions give me the insight I need into my company to make it the best possible. That's why I tell my ego to stand down. I don't need the title beside my name. I know who I am. What I am most interested in is promoting MCI, making my company the best possible. Keeping my neutral, flexible title on my cards keeps me grounded and focuses my attention on what is important—improving MCI and bringing it to the highest level.

Entrepreneurial 101 Takeaway:

1. *Remember that your title can open doors—and it can shut down the communication vital to you as an entrepreneur.*

2. *Choose a title that doesn't give away who you are— that lets you talk to everyone, from CEOs to the common man.*

CHAPTER 28:

When to Have Your Name in the Jingle

Having your name in the jingle is the flip side of having a neutral, flexible title on your business card. This is where I make it clear that I am President and Owner. Why? Because I'm not simply an employee of Mobile Cardiac Imaging. I can pull rank and say, "Look, my name is in the jingle. Yes, I do own the company." Used correctly and in the right situation, letting people know you're the owner—"having your name in the jingle"—opens doors to negotiate business quickly, right there on the spot. Having my name in the jingle means that I am a "get it done" kind of gal. You're not merely talking to an employee—you're talking to the decision-maker. The buck stops with me, and I am the decision-maker for the company.

There are distinct advantages to having your name in the jingle. It is clear that you are the person with whom clients will negotiate. You don't have to call back to the office to get the go-ahead. You are the one who can make the decision right then. There is no middleman between you and the person you're dealing with. The moment you make that "name in the jingle" statement, that allows others to know you are the decision-maker, the issue becomes doing business here and now, having people respond in the time frame that you want. It creates an avenue to make business happen quickly, professionally and efficiently.

The Decision-Maker Is Here, Ready to Do Business

You always want your name in the jingle—that instant recognition that you are the owner of the business—when you are negotiating with vendors, equipment manufacturers, and other people on that level. They know immediately that there are not going to be four or five callbacks. You don't need to talk back and forth with the company administrator. That vendor gets the immediate gratification of knowing, "I have the decision-maker, the policy-maker and the check-writer right here, all in one person." This allows me to broker deals right on the spot, how and when I want them made. Having your name in the jingle cuts all the red tape in doing business.

There are occasions where it is not to your advantage to have your name in the jingle when you are first starting out in business. Your business is new, you are unknown, and you may find that you need to fly under the radar. However, once you are established and the company is doing well, there is no disadvantage for having your name in the jingle. None. It just depends on how you choose to use that knowledge and when you choose to share it. Once your company becomes successful and your track record is good, it is always an advantage. You just pick and choose as to when you want to be identified as owner and decision maker. After a while, people identify you with your company—you become merged. I am merged with my company, and at the level of success we have achieved, it's always a good thing.

Entrepreneurial 101 Takeaway:

1. *Once your business is on track, put your name in the jingle—and keep it there.*

2. *Use the power of your "name in the jingle" to negotiate quickly, efficiently and on your own terms—you are the decision-maker!*

CHAPTER 29:

Keep Your Eyes on the Path—Not on the Prize

So often we hear people tell us to "keep your eyes on the prize." However, in business, that's not the best plan—in fact, it can derail you in your entrepreneurial pursuit. The prize that we often think we have to pursue consists of the awards, accolades and applause that will come if you do your job. The true entrepreneur focuses on the path—the journey to success. If you take your eyes off that path, that journey, you'll lose your focus and miss just where that journey is taking you.

In that business journey where you are developing your company and doing your homework, you'll encounter many forks in the road, trying to take you off the path one way or the other. The key is to not lose the focus of the journey you're on when you encounter pebbles in your shoes or boulders in your way. A major reason you need to keep your eyes on the path and not on the prize in the success you hope for, is that some forms of success will cause you to lose your focus and become misdirected.

I have had people approach me to buy MCI. As I've said, I'm moving toward an age where I'm considering looking for the next mountain to climb after MCI. They begin to talk with you about buying your company and you find yourself "getting ready" for departure. You start to get distracted because your focus is on Point X—the exit. Meanwhile, if you have lost your focus on the day-to-day path, your business sits and quivers. No, business must continue as long as you don't have a firm deal.

Don't Believe Your Own Press

Success often comes in the form of the award we win. Having won almost every award available, I am well aware that some of the awards and accolades are huge—and they can give you a false sense of "who you are." You start to think, *Wow! I'm an incredible human being!* You start believing your own press and begin to think that you are the award. You are the prize. No, that prize, that award or accolade, didn't get you to where you are today. You are where you are due to the path you have been on. You can't start pursuing the prize—you've got to focus on that path. Don't lose yourself to who people think you are. They don't know you. They don't know the battles you've waged to keep your business intact, to protect its foundation of integrity and ethical business practices. Don't let the glitz and the glamour of your awards and accolades pull your head up toward the clouds until your feet are no longer walking on the path. Instead, surround yourself with people who will keep you grounded.

I have a great staff—they keep me planted on a solid foundation. If I'm ever tempted to think that because of my awards and accolades I'm "all that," the next thing I know, one of my staff is in my office asking me to come look at a patient or at a scan or to start an IV line. My staff keeps me putting my feet on the path, one step at a time, one day at a time. I enjoy my awards—and you should enjoy yours—but I don't get overly impressed with them. I don't want to lose what I started with.

Keep Working Your Day Job

Some entrepreneurs achieve their success early—too early. They have never had to wear the ten to fifteen hats that most of us remember from our early days starting our companies. The temptation can be strong to focus on the good times of success rather than the hard work it took to achieve that success. Other entrepreneurs find while they were building their personal and company images, they suddenly became the "hot commodity" in their industry. The next thing they know, they are invited out everywhere. With that much running around, when are you going to focus on the path? Be selective with your time. You have a day job—your business. Don't forget the day-to-day journey that your business provides.

Those hot commodities who lose sight of time for the path remind me of the author Truman Capote. He achieved the high pinnacle of success when he published his novel, *In Cold Blood*. This was what he had worked a lifetime for, and he became the hot ticket, invited to parties and talk shows. He forgot his own "day job" and never wrote a significant novel again. Be sure you have real friends who can help you down the ladder of being the latest thing and back onto your path. Let those friends, family and the people closest to you help you stay focused.

Watch out how you use the word "success." Use it sparingly. If I still see success as something to come, something to work for, I am likely to stay on the path. Running a business is tough work. If you are going to run that business, staying on the path, you will have to grow a tough skin. As a woman, I learned that I have to use my voice and presence to command respect. I learned that the "girl" doesn't survive in a tough, competitive business world. The girl has to stay home, and the woman has to show up every day. That woman has to stay focused to keep the level of achievement she has won.

How do you keep your focus on the path when everything else is competing for your time and attention? Surround yourself with real people who have your best interests at heart. Make sure they are positive people who can encourage you and walk the path with you without inflating your ego. My husband and family are just that kind of people. Believe me, when I'm cooking dinner after a long day, or cleaning house, or helping my son with his needs, I come right back down to earth. My staff also helps me stay focused on the path. "Colleen, can you come start an IV?" They keep me grounded in the world of my business, reminding me that it's not about the prize—it's about the path.

You will have to work to keep the real you—the internal you— grounded. You can help yourself by staying focused, determined and goal-oriented. Examine that path you're on—look for the next step, the next project to complete, the next mountain to climb. Look around the corner at the path and where it's taking you!

Entrepreneurial 101 Takeaway:

1. *The "prize" didn't get you where you are today—and it's not going to take you where you need to go.*

2. *Focus on walking your path—build your business, bring passion and excellence to what you're doing.*

3. *As a small business owner, you'll have more interaction with your staff. Let that interaction work to keep you focused on the daily path.*

CHAPTER 30:

Never Less Than My Best

It all started when I opened the doors of my company. I decided that this company would have the best—and even more—that my money could buy. I saw what other facilities were doing, and I decided to make it better. I took the best I could find, and I improved on it. When you walk into my facility, it's like walking into someone's home. It's beautiful. It doesn't look like a hospital or a clinic. It looks like a luxury spa. I did that on purpose.

Don't Spend $5 When You Have $10

Always give your best in terms of how your facility looks. No one is ever going to let you forget the details you missed. Pay close attention to them. Choose the best fabrics, the most elegant designs. When you first open your business, you will be painfully aware that you can't compete with the big boys. Even if you have some areas where you are competitive with them, you know that you can't compete with them in every arena. Know your weaknesses. I bought the best equipment I could afford when I started

MCI, but there was no way that I could afford a $2.5 million scanner. Instead, I had a $1 million one that performed just as good, gave the same reports and worked just as well. I couldn't bring my equipment up to the level I wanted immediately, but I bought the best we could afford.

Then, I made the rest of our facility the best I could. I imported the carpet and furniture from out of state. Could I have bought them in Tulsa—and much cheaper? Yes, but I would know every single day that I entered through the doors that I didn't "make the rest the best."

It's easy to confuse the "best" with perfection. Trying to achieve perfection will drive you over the edge. The "best" however will create a cycle of positive energy in your facility. I don't allow mistakes to continue. I come to work each day and give my best. I ask my staff to give their best, and that passion and enthusiasm travel like wildfire. I come in each morning, thinking, *I've got it. I'm the leader here.* Remember, you set the tone. When I walk in the door each morning, I am determined to give my best. I look at my facility, and it is the very best I can make it—the most beautiful, the most elegant, the most efficient.

The Girl Has Got to Stay at Home

I have also found that in order to be at my competitive best, I need to set the "girl stuff" aside. I leave "home" at home. I always say, "The girl needs to stay at home. There's no place for her here." If I'm sick, you won't know it. Or if I have a problem, you're never going to know anything about that. I give my best every morning, every afternoon, every day. When I give my best, my staff is challenged to give their best. When I leave at night, I know that whatever faced me, whatever I had to do or had to fix, I gave it my best. I did the best that I could do. The positive energy this produces is phenomenal!

Entrepreneurial 101 Takeaway:

1. *Make your facility the most attractive and appealing it can be—buy the best your money will let you buy.*

2. *Give your best effort every time—as a leader, you set the tone for your business.*

3. *Women—make the girl stay at home. Your best requires the strong businesswoman to show up every day.*

CHAPTER 31:

Remember to Remember (Rituals to Help)

One of the valuable tools for the small business entrepreneur is the collection of rituals that help you stay focused and on your path. I found early that I needed to make a point of setting time aside, to remember what is important about my business, and to remember the details that I need to stay on top of my company.

When I first opened the doors of MCI, I did not have a personal assistant. I had one employee, my administrator. I couldn't afford an assistant. Several years later, I talked to a man who was also a new business owner. He had not established his business yet. He hardly had furniture or a computer—but he had hired a personal assistant! There was nothing to "assist," but he had an assistant anyway. He hired someone to help him remember his business before there *was* any business. Women and men function very differently in business.

My Day Is Just Starting

When I started out with MCI, I realized that with so many people pulling on me all day long, wanting my help, needing my input, how could I remember all the details that I needed to run my business? I couldn't write everything down. I started "working to remember" every day—remembering phone numbers that I needed, contracts that I was pursing or getting ready to sign, significant people whose names and faces I needed to know. I decided to make a point of remembering every day. I focused on keeping the projects of the day on my brain, because I had an open-door policy that left me to do most of my work from 5:00 to 7:00 P.M. When my employees left for the day, that was when my day started.

During that time, I would stop and reflect on my day. I'd make a point of categorizing items in my mind. This was my personal time where I did *my* job. I took time to "remember to remember." During the day, I dealt with the issues facing my employees. Every time one of them came into my office and interrupted the flow of what I was doing, I would have an eight to ten minute conversation, followed by that fifteen minutes to get myself back on track. Each interruption cost me about twenty-five minutes out of my day. Just a few interruptions, and my morning or afternoon was shot. I found that during my time in the evening, I needed to remember just to do my job!

Someone at the Helm

As an on-site business owner, you have much more involvement in the day-to-day running of your company. When do you find time to actually run your business? Someone needs to be at the helm. I have to make the time to remember what needs to be done for my business. I do write down some items, I use my calendar and my voice recorder—but I also use my mind, my memory, to remember what needs to be done.

My ritual of reflecting and categorizing at the end of the day is my way of remembering to remember what I need to do, why I need to do it and what my business is all about. Create a habit, a ritual, that allows you to focus on what is most important in your business, that allows you to "be at the helm" of your company. Rituals to help you focus on your business keep the business from running you, and ensure that you are always running the business.

Entrepreneurial 101 Takeaway:

1. *Create your own ritual—a time, a place—to reflect on the day.*

2. *Use your calendar, voice recorder, etc.—but work on keeping details in your head. They make you "remember" why you're in business.*

CHAPTER 32:

Live Your Life Today for Where You Are Tomorrow

You can't live in the past, and you can't live in the future. Live your best life today—enjoy the moment you're in. I have found that when you live in the future, trying to fulfill the requirements of a business plan, or in the past, regretting what has happened, you create unnecessary stress in your life.

Instead, live in the present and know that the results will come. Remove the false expectations of trying to live in the future. Instead, focus on one day at a time. As I like to say, "Do today, tomorrow will take care of itself." Too many women live under a burden of unrealistic expectations. Instead, make a point of living in the now. Do the best job you can for today. Tomorrow will come. Focus on where you are today—let today be your primary goal. And the future? How you get there depends on what you do now.

What You Do Today Brings Your Tomorrow

Keep your focus on the day-to-day path of your business and your life. When you lose your focus and begin to look at what you should be doing in the future, or what you might be doing, the pressure of "tomorrow" takes away your joy and the fun of building your business. It creates a cumulative sense of failure. This failure becomes a powerful psychological tool. You can turn yourself into a self-made failure.

Or, you can realize that today is not the same day that yesterday was. Come with the excitement of facing the unexpected. I made a decision many years ago not to live under the burden of the future. I had drawn up an original business plan—my banker had it. He would not let me off the "path" that the business plan had marked out for me. The pressure of that plan—the false expectations it set up—combined to try to take away the passion and fun of running my company. Instead, I decided to leave that path. I began to walk down my own path, to strike out on my own path and take a chance. This doesn't work just for your business—it works for your life. I have faced the "boulders" in life—the biggest obstacles as times change. Do I diversify? Equipment is cheaper— do I stay in mobile environment? Do I transition into another field? What am I supposed to do next?

The best answer to these questions is to keep my focus on today, on the task at hand. As I focus on what lies before me, tomorrow will come. The way I reach tomorrow is to focus on what I am doing now.

Entrepreneurial 101 Takeaway:

1. *Concentrate on the now.*
2. *Enjoy the moment—it is what will take you to your tomorrow.*

CHAPTER 33:

Be Clear

When you are dealing with so many people, when they are pulling at you in the course of the day on your entrepreneurship road, the message you are trying to get across often gets confused. As an entrepreneur, when I am venturing out in so many different directions, I tend to be very much on the go—quick with details, quick with directions and responses. I believe that in the midst of this, you need to stop, take a moment and be very "clear" as to what directions you are giving.

Early in my journey, I'd give out directions to my staff and because they didn't want to bother me, because I appeared to be scattered and going a mile a minute, they'd go off thinking I had said one thing, and it would be wrong. They would take something I said in passing, and it wouldn't be what I meant at all. Because of my aggressive personality and because I was the owner, my staff wouldn't come back for clarification. I saw this over and over, thinking, *Is there something wrong with my delivery? Have I created a climate of fear for my staff where they are afraid to come back and ask, "What did you say?"*

Sometimes when you are watching or observing other CEOs, you see this dynamic over and over. You can sit in the same boardroom and wonder what people are talking about. You question what is being said—and half the people in there don't have a clue what the speaker is saying either. The next thing you know, everyone leaves the office, gets into a huddle and tries to assess and evaluate what was said and what action is needed. Everyone offers their own interpretation and by the time they are done, it's like that game of gossip where you whisper a statement down a line of twenty people. By the time it reaches the last person, it doesn't bear any resemblance to the original statement.

Change the Climate in Your Office

I address this problem by encouraging my staff to come back if necessary and ask me what I meant. "If you are unsure what it was I said, or what I meant, I want to be *very clear* with you so we are on the same page and your direction is not hindered." The only way I can get that across is by constantly reinforcing the idea of "being clear." I use that phrase daily in my company. I want to "be clear" in my communication. I want you to "be clear" as to what I mean. I want you to have the correct interpretation of what it is I said. If you don't understand what I meant, feel free to come back and ask me again.

That isn't always easy for your employees to do. Sometimes there is such an intimidation and fear factor of coming back to whoever is in charge and asking, "What exactly did you mean? What was it that you said?" Being clear with your employees, with your clients, with everyone you communicate with is an important part of your entrepreneur journey. I emphasize over and over to my staff that I want to *be clear* with them, and I want them to feel comfortable in asking me again what I said and meant.

Creating an atmosphere without intimidation or fear isn't easy. As long as you wear the title of CEO or President, people are naturally going to feel uncomfortable about asking what you meant and requesting you to repeat yourself. After all, you hold their jobs in your hands. One thing that I do is have an open-door policy where my office door is constantly open. I allow my staff to communicate with me directly. I try to encourage them to come to me when they have questions or are confused by what I meant.

Unfortunately, subordinates may not lose that fear of asking you to repeat yourself. At the end of the day, it's your name on their paycheck, it's your company where they are working. The sense that someone can lose his or her job on a whim doesn't seem to go away. No matter how good a working relationship you have with your staff, they don't completely lose that sense that you hold control over them. That is why I think it is important to "be clear" with your employees, to allow them to ask questions, to tell them that they have the opportunity to come back and ask you for clarification.

Sharpen Your Delivery to Instill Confidence

How can you as an entrepreneur avoid some of the fear factor with your employees? I am convinced that about 75 percent of intimidation comes from your delivery. In running a multimillion dollar company, you have so much running through your head in terms of your operation that you have limited time to talk to your employees. If you have more than five or six people working for you, on any given day, each one of them may be vying for your time—along with your business partners, vendors and clients until your day threatens to run over into the next one! You have a three- to five-minute window to tell me what you need to say. Too often, people want to take the "long route"—they want to go around the corner, down the block and back up the street. What I need is a "nuts and bolts" version—tell me you're at the street corner and what happened there.

Consequently, when I respond, I am moving at top speed because they have exceeded their "window." I find myself talking fast and ending with, "Do you understand?" And my employees, realizing that there is now a time issue, usually say, "Okay, I understand"—even when they don't. I have to watch how I respond to them—my tone, my expression, my attitude—so they don't get stuck in saying, "Yes, I've got it" when they don't know what I want.

The best advice I can give the new entrepreneur is to work on your delivery so that you first of all communicate your vision clearly. Be concise and speak on a level each person can under-stand. I find that takes studying and knowing my employees—and it's all a part of being able to communicate to any group of people. You also need to communicate that asking for clarification is perfectly okay. I make a point of taking a moment and really looking at the person I'm speaking with to make sure that they are hearing and understanding. Then I ask, "Are you *clear?*" Somehow, that statement acts as a code. My employees have come to realize that I'm asking them if they really understood me, if I really communicated. It tells them that it's all right to ask questions, to get me to explain again, until they *are* clear. Their answer also gives me a level of confidence. It lets me know that I have taken enough time to deliver what they need to accomplish their job and given them the time they need to process my directions.

"Being Clear"—A Win/Win Situation

Learning to communicate clearly—*being clear*—isn't a skill you pick up in a single day. It develops over time; it's a part of your entrepreneur journey. And the communication isn't just on your part. When I ask someone if they are *clear,* I've given them a way to communicate back to me. I've found that timing is everything. When they are right there with me, it's easier to ask me for clarification than it is for them to go away, realize they don't know what to do and then have to come see me again. It saves time for both of us.

When we are "in the moment," it's like we're having a question-and-answer seminar. But if they walk away, not knowing what I meant, their imagination starts up. They begin to think that if they walk back in, interrupt me to say, "I guess I didn't really understand you," it sets up negativity in your employees that destroys their positive approach to work. And again, I can't stress the time that I've saved not having to interrupt what I'm doing, explain again and then try to get back on track.

Listen to Your Staff—Listen to Yourself

I have found that "being clear" involves listening. First, I have to listen to my staff in terms of knowing whether or not they understood me. Second, I have to remind myself that what is clear to me as a communicator may not be clear to the listener. It's easy to think, *He/she wasn't listening. She didn't listen to me.* But an employee can be listening closely, and the problem doesn't lie with them. You may be the difficulty. Stop frequently and assess yourself: Was I being clear with this employee? Was my communication clear? That is significant in itself. Part of the responsibility of the entrepreneur is to learn to make your directives understandable to the person hearing them and give them an opportunity to get you to clarify. If this isn't your best skill yet, remember that the entrepreneur life is a journey. You grow and develop—and it's to your advantage in every way to develop this area of your 101 skills.

Entrepreneur 101 Takeaway:

1. *Make your directions concise, speaking on that person's level.*

2. *Give your staff time to process the information, and the opportunity to ask for clarification on the spot.*

3. *Use certain phrases, watching your attitude and expression, to communicate that asking for clarification is not just acceptable—it's desirable!*

CHAPTER 34:

Clarity Produces Confidence

Clarity and confidence are linked to each other. Every day I come to work, I create an environment where my agenda is not so full of "stuff" that I don't have one free cell of my brain left to stay on top of what's going on. On any given day, true entrepreneurs have all kinds of ideas running around in their minds—you have to slow them down and put them in a corner where you can grab the one you need for that day. Each morning when I come to work, I need to have a clear head—my clarity has to be such that when I enter the office, I might have twenty projects going on, but each one has to be in the right place for me to put my hands on it at the right time.

My brain, to me, is like a bookshelf. You know a certain book is there. You can read it anytime you want, but it has to be placed on the shelf, out of the way, until I am ready to actually pull it off and read it. It's the same way with keeping my clarity. I have learned to focus on one thing at a time. I'm project-driven, but it's one project at a time. I don't allow my head to fill up with the clutter of many projects when I'm focusing on one of them. I put the other projects "up on the shelf"—they'll be there when it's time to pull them down and forge ahead with them.

If you don't have this clarity and focus, you can't have the confidence you need in business. Sometimes people come to my office talking to me about their business ventures. Often, they have five or six different ventures going on, but not one is successful. They have their thoughts so scattered that they can't focus on the one at hand.

Don't Lose Your Focus

You have to concentrate on one thing—just one. Make one venture, that one idea, work for you. Now you can go on to the second one. By the time your business is established, you'll have developed the skill set to apply your time and energy to several projects. In the beginning, however, have one project. Do a great job on it. The level of success from that will give you the confidence to say, "I can carry out something else!"

I try to mentor people in terms of their vision. I had an entrepreneur come in about six months ago. I never take anyone's vision away from them, but this young man sat before me with six projects in his head. He wanted to start them all at one time. I told him that he needed to go back to the drawing board, sit still for a while and figure out just what it was he was doing. He needed to decide which project had the most significance to him, which one had the best chance of success. If he tried to start up all his projects at the same time, there is no way he could have the success rate that would build his confidence to take on new ventures.

Confidence is part of the journey—it builds from success to success. It enables you to hit that "ceiling" and push beyond it.

As women, we're generally multitaskers. I want to emphasize something about multitasking. It's a great ability to have. I hire multitaskers, but I have them use those skills in the service of *one* project at a time. I don't ask them—and I don't ask myself—to try to keep a string of different projects going at one time. That's the worst way to use your multitasking skills, especially when you are starting out in business. What will happen is that you will not be able to create success in any area—your failures will drown you. Instead of trying to accomplish half a dozen projects at one time, pick the one project that will yield the best results. Apply your multitasking skills to that one project. Allow your successes to build up rather than failures. Success building on top of success equals confidence for those bigger projects that lie ahead on your path.

The Journey to Confidence

When I started MCI, I didn't have the confidence I needed. I was a good nuclear medicine technologist, but that didn't give me the confidence to run a multimillion dollar company when I had never "run" anything other than my basic $50,000 paycheck. Like anyone else, each time I made a decision that worked, my confidence built. Over time, you come to a point where no matter what decisions face you, you give off the sense that you can do this, you can face it, make the right decisions and bring success. You exude that confidence to those around you. Some people mistake it for arrogance, but it's not. When I talk to you, I will tell you what I can do, what I'm good at—it's not to be offensive or cocky. It's because I can actually do those things. I have confidence that has developed over the course of my journey.

There are a couple of things that I know that I am very good at and I can back it up with action, and that is where my confidence began to build. Speak it, and let the results speak for themselves.

I want to address some issues that specifically face the woman entrepreneur in this area of confidence. Our training as women, the way we're often raised—especially in the South where I'm from— tells us that we need to be polite, and somewhat refined or "lady-like" when we push ourselves forward and say, "I'm good at this!" Once again, that girl needs to stay at home—she can't be showing up in the business arena. If you're a woman reading this, realize that it's important for you to speak about your skills, what you're good at doing. It builds your confidence.

Women particularly need that confidence in the business arena—for too many years it has been a "boys only" club. Historically, women haven't been able to say, "I'm good at this!" Men have had that freedom. If a man is a welder, and he's good at that, he's expected to say so. If a man is a truck driver and he can park that truck anywhere, drive it anywhere, he's allowed to say so. For women, that hasn't always been the case. However, there are positive changes taking place. Recently, I saw a female attorney on TV who made it clear that she was good, saying, "I'm one of the best attorneys in Houston!" What comes across in a man as confidence and assurance is sometimes called arrogance and aggression in women. And sometimes it's called worse things.

Speak Your Success

Women, toughen up! There have been two sets of rules—one for men, one for women. I am convinced that if women stepped out more, and said, "Here's what I can do. I'm good at it!" this would breed a more positive approach for us in business. It's time to stop being the "pushovers" of our own success. Women will fight hard for their husbands' success, they will make sure everyone knows they are good at what they do, but when it comes to their own ability, they sometimes lie down and roll over. They work on pushing their children forward, raising their self-esteem and confidence, but they ignore their own need for confidence.

When you hear the statement, "I'm good at this," the chances are about 80 percent that it is a man who has said this. Should men stop speaking about their abilities and successes? Of course not! It's just that women need to step up to the plate and start building their own confidence. None of us are born with that level of confidence we need to achieve all of our dreams.

The confident entrepreneur is developed over time. If you're not confident, you can become confident. It's part of that entrepreneur journey. Deep within each of us is the sense that we are capable, that we have ability and talent. For the developing entrepreneur—especially for the woman entrepreneur—it's just a matter of bringing it to light, acknowledging that that ability is there and learning how to use it. Over time, you learn how to "bring out" that tremendously confident woman and put her to work for you. Do you need to walk around with that assertive— some would say aggressive—chip on your shoulder all the time?

No, all it will do is cause you emotional stress, draining you of energy that your business needs.

But should you walk around with the quiet, mild-mannered woman in evidence all the time? No! Like most areas of entrepreneurship, it's all a matter of balancing the assertive decision maker with the nurturing mother. Most women, whether they actually are mothers or not, have a strong "mother instinct" about them. You simply need to pick and choose which woman shows up. You make that decision based upon which one is needed at the moment!

Do you need to walk around with that mild-mannered woman all the time? No. But you have to be able to balance the aggressor, the controller, against the mother instinct. You have to pick who comes with you each day, who you "bring out." Most of the time, the one you "bring out" is yourself—the person you are 80 percent of the time. This is the person you function with every day. There are times, however, that you do need to function with compassion. When you function as the business owner, people sometimes forget that you can be compassionate, too.

Recently, I had a meeting, and because I'm both a business owner and also a female, people constantly want to tell me stories that they wouldn't tell a man in my position. "My children are sick, so I'm going to be late for work" or "I can't come in today." "I had to go shop for groceries so it will delay this or that." Finally, I had to tell my staff that honestly, that's personal and has nothing to do with your job. Sometimes they forget that I'm an employer and they weigh me down with all of their personal issues. I'm concerned with their job and the quality of the position, because at the end of the day, I'm the employer.

I Don't Care

Many of them saw that as a terribly harsh statement, and it bothered them more because some of my staff have referred to me as Mother Love—I am the one who makes sure that everyone's life is going well. That's a compliment—but it can also be a detriment. As good as it is for me to be concerned about you because I am a woman with that compassionate side, it's also possible for people to try to take advantage of it. I finally had to decide that I didn't care about their personal lives because that becomes overwhelming. What I did care about was the time my staff put in on their jobs. I had to communicate to them that they had become overly confident and presumptuous with me simply because I am a woman. I had to get the idea across that it didn't matter who was sick in their families. This is business. I never come to work and tell my staff anything about my child—no matter what is going on with him.

And of course, my saying this just crushed people because I'm a woman—and I'm supposed to care. What I realized was that I was hearing so many stories about my staff's problems, while I knew that a man in this position would never sit at this desk and hear all of this or be taken advantage of in this way. Every so often, I have to let them know that what matters is that they come to work and do their jobs. What happens outside doesn't concern me. I just want to know one thing: Are you doing your job? I have too much going on inside my mind to take on your problems, so don't tell me these things anymore.

As a business owner, this made sense. But my staff saw it as being cruel and unfeeling because they wanted me to be "female friendly"—and I can't *always* be female friendly. This is part of the balance that I have to keep as a business owner. I do care about my staff—but I have to balance that in terms of their work with them being there. Most of the time, I function as who I am— Colleen Payne-Nabors, businesswoman. But inside of me are these "other women" that I can bring with me. They show up when they are needed. If I need that tough, hard businesswoman, she can show up. If there is a moment where there really does need to be that compassion, that compassionate, nurturing woman can show up. It's all a matter of keeping these women in balance, and making sure the *right* one comes to work with me that day.

How do I know this? It's because early on, when I first started my business, those women didn't show up when they should. They appeared inappropriately—and would hang around for weeks or even months. In my earliest days, I remember that that compassionate woman showed up about 90 percent of the time. She came to work with me almost every day. That was the woman who wanted to be the caregiver, who wanted to look after the men, the woman who was the "nice gal"—she came to work way too often and stayed for far too long. She caused me a great many problems.

Who Came to Work with You Today?

And sometimes, her alter ego showed up—the aggressor-over-achiever, the hard woman. She really stayed too long—and if you're a woman, you really can't afford for her to be there on a permanent basis. She's aggressive—she'll cause emotional distress and hypertension and heart palpitations. She can send you into depression. Our bodies just can't take that woman being around too often. I found that the nurturing woman would show up, caring and compassionate, and if I didn't watch out for her, she'd put me out of business. I had to get tough. The next day, I'd pull out the tough gal, and say, "Let's go to work and handle things." That tough gal stayed around for over a year. She allowed that woman that I really am to stay in business!

However, once I realized that "she" had made her point, that people could no longer walk in my office, slam my door, tell me off and do craziness like that, balance came. The aggressor and the compassionate woman learned to get into balance with the woman I am. I had to achieve balance—my compassionate woman was letting people just run over me. I was miserable. I'd think, *This is a great job! Why are you ruining it for me?* I'd just wonder when this trouble was going to be over—how much longer I would have to endure it. The truth was that it would be over when I brought the right woman to work and put an end to it—and not before!

Family Business Is Hard Business

I had a situation going on that many women in business face. I had relatives working for me—several relatives. Unfortunately, I found that they were coming in and running the company for me. I had to fire all but one. That made going home to visit difficult, but I had to protect my business. Very early in my company's history, I had one of my brothers, Jeremy, driving for me. He would return to the office from driving the truck, lie on the office couch and go to sleep. My other employees would come to me, saying, "He's so cute out there asleep!" their way of letting me know that he was in the patient lobby asleep on the couch and the aggressive woman had to go out there and handle the situation.

No One Goes Toe-to-Toe

Women! Working with family is extremely difficult. My baby sister, and you know what they say about the baby, Angela, started to work with me around five years ago. She'd come to work, have a bad day and walk in my office to announce what she *wasn't going to do* and how she *wasn't going to do it.* She had such a strong personality, and I'd think, *Oh my God, this is awful.* I'd get on the phone, call my mother, and say, "Mom, you have got to tell her to stop this, or she can't come to work anymore." I didn't feel that I could fire her. Instead, I'd call my sisters and ask, "Could you all please talk to her because she is just killing me!"

One day, I realized that *she* was running me and my company! She felt she had the right to be ugly to other employees because I was letting her get away with being ugly to me. I made a decision: no more. It was time to pull the aggressive woman off the shelf and put her to work. Angela was my family, but she didn't own my company. The next time she came into my office, screaming at me at the top of her lungs, I stood up, walked over and shut the door, turned around and told her, "I have had enough! You didn't start this company with me. You may not finish with me, so here's how it's going to be. You are going to get your backside out of my office!"

I drew the line in the sand. No one gets to stand toe-to-toe with me and challenge me—not when my name is on the bottom of their check. No one gets to "win" in my office but me. If you challenge me, you had better *come with it,* because I am always going to win. I don't mean that my employees can't give me their opinions and input—I mean that no one challenges my authority as the owner of my company. We had about a year of that kind of drama, and that day, I put an end to it. She still has an aggressive personality—that's just how my family is—but she doesn't get to use that with me.

At that time, however, I only fixed part of the problem. After that initial episode, she came up with her own "rule" that from 8:00 to 5:00 she worked for me, and after 5:00, we became family so she could come in and talk with me anyway she wanted. I put up with that for about six months and decided, "This isn't working for me either! I still sign your checks. You don't get to act that way with me." This was part of my journey—a painful part—where I learned that I had to bring the right woman to work with me to control various daily situations.

Balance in Who Comes to Work

I realized that in situations like that, I couldn't bring that compassionate woman to work, because she didn't have it in her to make the hard decisions. She is the one who just "goes along" with whatever is happening. I had to bring the aggressor out who would kick their butts and take names. She was the one I needed to get the job done. Finally, I realized that I could merge the three women— the "real me," the aggressor and the nurturer. I could put them on the shelf, figure out who was needed when and then bring her out. I also learned that part of balance was being able to bring the woman I really am—the woman I am every day—out most of the time every day. I want that woman operating with me in the "now" that I operate in, every single day.

Entrepreneurial 101 Takeaway:

1. *Pick the project that has the best immediate chance of success, that will bring the highest reward for right now—and focus on it.*

2. *Stay in the now—don't get distracted by the projects you want to do in the future.*

3. *Let each small success lead the way to more successes— success multiplied over produces confidence.*

4. *Know that as a woman, you are going to have to bring the "tough woman" to work with you—and learn when to bring her out, and when to put her up.*

5. *Growing into a strong, confident leader is part of the journey. Even if you think your personality doesn't fit that "tough woman" role—you can develop that side of yourself and use her when you need to.*

CHAPTER 35:

You Never Win If You Only Take: What Are You Giving Back?

In every area of your life, you can't just take; you have to give back. The reason so many companies are successful is that they contribute to the community. Would you always go to Wal-Mart if the organization constantly took and never gave to any charitable organization? You still need their services, but it's wonderful to know that at Christmastime they donate so many gifts to people in need. Target makes a point of publishing the things it does corporately in order to say, "Not only are we *in* your community, but we are a *part* of your community. And we are giving back to it."

You Have Something to Give

MCI is not one of the largest companies, but we have to invest something in our community. No, we are not Target, and we are not Wal-Mart. But I have learned this lesson—in order to win, to have real success and not just a great balance sheet, you have to be a part of where you live. You have to give your time, your energy and your money back to the people who allow you to be in business.

I make sure that we share everything we can; we share services that we provide with the indigent. We carry out projects for individuals. I donate time and mentor people. The way in which you give back depends on who you are as a person, your personality and on the place you are in your entrepreneurial journey. You want to be able to do something for those around you that says, "Not only was this person a successful business owner, but they made the world a better place!"

What Is Your Legacy?

What is it you leave behind? Besides running a successful business, what else is there? In terms of making you a well-rounded person in the context of your venture, you must give back. In some sense, it doesn't matter so much what you are giving as long as you *are* giving. You become a better person when you give. It's not that you give to get recognition; you give because it is the right thing to do. You give, because others need you to give to them. And you need to give back as well.

In my business arena, we come across so many people who are indigent or who work but don't have insurance. How can we give to them? We have tests that are expensive—so much so that people without insurance can't afford them. We work with physicians who call us and say, for example, "I have a patient who really needs a MRI scan. Is there a way you can help us?"

Yes, we can help. We work with several of the colleges in town who treat indigent and uninsured patients. Sometimes people have a low level of insurance with no coverage for diagnostic proce-dures. Because my company provides high-end procedures, we can give back by donating them. Whatever industry you operate in, you can find a way to give. If you own a bakery, you can give food to the homeless or to various shelters.

Because It's the Right Thing to Do

Here at MCI, we have adopted families and set up Christmas programs to help them provide for their families at the holiday season. I have helped save other businesses. People have come to me in their time of need, and while I don't generally disclose the details, I have been able to help many people. I don't use the occa-sions I give to gain an advantage in business. I never tell the specific ways I help individuals because I don't think that's what giving really is. People come and ask for help; it's not right of me to say, "This is what my company did." But thanks to the financial success I have had in my business, I have been able to help buy vehicles for people who need to get around, I've been able to keep the lights on and pay the rent when people have had their backs up against the wall. I find that what we have helped people do is simply incredible—I had no idea that my business would allow me to help on this scale.

We have given to many charitable organizations, to various churches, even in various situations. In every business, in every arena, there are multitudes of ways to give back. And it's not for recognition. You already have recognition for your business. You give because you get to make a difference and help others who are in despair and in need. As a mentor to young entrepreneurs, I talk constantly about giving back to those around you. I remind them of the positive way it makes them better people, better citizens in their communities.

Giving Is the Key to Growth

There is a negative part of giving as well. When there are relatively few people giving back, you become a target. Everyone comes to you, and you have to know when not to give, when to say "no." However, I find overall that giving is a part of the inner spiritual development, if you will, that is necessary to a business owner. It is part of what you must do so you can grow. You give, and your company grows. You give, and you grow as a person. The services that my business provides make a difference, but when I give to others out of what we have, there is a deeper level of feeling we make a significant difference in the lives of other people.

When I provide services as part of my business, I expect monetary gain. But when I give back to the community, I'm not looking to make money. What we do is an act of the heart, the giving of human to human. It doesn't bring in money, but what it produces in our lives and in the lives of others is so worthwhile that no monetary value can be placed on it.

Entrepreneurial 101 Takeaway:

1. *The business that is successful in those intangible ways that define success is the one that gives back to the community.*

2. *Within your business itself lie the seeds of what you can give. The services or goods you provide for profit can be used to help people who have nothing, who can't help themselves, who need what you have.*

3. *You don't give for recognition. You give because it's the right thing to do. When you do this, you and your business will grow in all the ways that matter.*

CHAPTER 36:

Mentoring— Giving to Get Back

Right now, "mentoring" is a hot topic. It's one of those words that everyone wants to use, wants to be associated with. When I first started this company, I didn't have a mentor. There was no one I could go to for references, no one who could give me contacts for my business. There were a couple of doctors who helped me because I was in the medical arena along with them, but once I began to have some success, that stopped. They were great guys—they helped me a great deal, but once I was on my way, the advice came to an end. I didn't have anyone to sit with and discuss my business ideas and all of the craziness that I faced every day.

And early on, no one came to me to be mentored. People want mentors who have proven themselves successful. I don't think you can mentor anyone until you have a proven record of success in some arena. However, as my level of success in my industry grew, I would find that a couple of times a month, someone would approach me to mentor them. I might be out speaking in the community, and someone would ask if I could be their mentor. You want to help other young entrepreneurs who are facing the obstacles you faced, but you can't mentor everyone. If you spend all your time investing into others, how can you continue to be successful? I find that I have to protect my personal and private time because after I would speak somewhere, a number of women would always approach me afterward asking for my guidance.

Finding the Right Person to Mentor

However, I have had the opportunity of mentoring one woman of whom I'm very proud. Risha Grant is the business editor of *Exposure* magazine. Early in my career, just after I won my very first award, she was an up-and-coming editor. We happened to take the same airline flight, and we began to talk. It just so happened that she was instrumental in getting several articles written about me. I have been able to mentor her and assist her in various practical ways. I did this because so much of what she had experienced was similar to—and in some instances, much more difficult—than what I had known as a new businesswoman. I had had no path marked out for me, I had walked that journey alone and I knew that what I had learned on my journey could help another businessperson.

Of course, Risha isn't the only person I have mentored. But she is the one I'm most proud of. I have mentored others and find that about every other month, someone wants to come by my office and discuss a business deal that they hope to put together. Many of them believe that I have some special key to success. The first thing I tell them is that the key to success is just plain old hard work, knowing that you can make it, not letting failure be an option and not looking too far down the road. I tell them, "Stay where you are and stay focused."

I no longer go to lunch or dinner with clients. About six years ago, I stopped doing that because I realized that it just wasn't part of who I am. Too often, people use lunch or dinner as a way to delay business. I stopped having lunch and dinner meetings because this was not a productive arena for me. If it's business we need to discuss, then let's do business. I prefer business in my office and that's not saying I will not come to your office—I will, but I will not go out to eat with you. It's just one of the rules by which I live my life. If business is going to be conducted, it can be conducted in the office environment. This is also due to me being very protective of my time. This process has worked for me, but it may not work for you.

Trust me, it's difficult to tell clients that you don't do lunch or dinner. So, I've learned if lunch or dinner is important to the relationship of our meeting, then I cater lunch or dinner into our office. Our conference room is beautiful—I built our office to be able to cater these lunches or dinners into my office. It's just my way of doing necessary business and learning to do it my way—and I save time by not going out. If you want to do business with me, I'll come to your office, and we'll hammer out our deal. Lunch and business may mix for some people, but not for me.

You Can't Mentor Everyone—Choose Carefully

One young man who wanted me to mentor him told me that he liked to go to lunch and dinner with his clients. My first response was, "Who pays for all of that? That's a whole lot of money right there." And my second response was, "If you take an hour-and-a-half every day to go to lunch, you also had to take fifteen or twenty minutes to get to those lunch appointments and another fifteen or twenty minutes to get back."

"Do you have two hours every day to lose?" I asked when he said he went to lunch every day with someone. Then he told me that on Fridays he played golf. I thought, *Man! You are living in a fantasy world!* His business wasn't successful, and he came to ask for advice on how to become a successful business owner. He obviously had read the fantasy book for entrepreneurs, the one that says, "My time is my time. I have other people working for me. They might not be doing a good job, but this is how I run my company. I can go golfing if I want because it's my company!"

He wanted to have other meetings with me, but we never did again. I just said that he probably lost fifteen hours a week just going to lunch. And he took a day off to go golfing when he was just starting out. He wanted the success before his business was successful. Success would come. His problem was that everything he did was the opposite of what makes an entrepreneur successful in business.

Mentoring is one way of giving back, but you have to be careful who you choose and the time you give to them. I couldn't invest in this young man because his entrepreneur style was so different from my style, and it wasn't a mentoring match. If he had to go to lunch with clients every day, had to go golfing on Friday—he and I were not going to be on the same page. I am a workaholic and although that doesn't necessarily mean you need to be, there does need to be something that I can pull from you and help nurture. There needs to be the potential for growth because mentoring is a partnership.

Are You Going in the Same Direction?

I still take people to mentor. If you just want a couple of hours to come in and run your thoughts by me, that's fine. In terms of mentoring over time, however, I have to pick the correct person. It needs to be the one who is on a success path, one whom I can help. I have to know that my time and advice are not going to be wasted. I might want to help you, but if you can't put my advice into practice, then can I really help you?

Another person I mentored had a great business going, but they were being pulled in every direction. Everyone wanted them to be at their function, at this event and that event. Every night, this person was out at a different event. They ran their business well, but the problem is that you just can't be out every single night. You have to level with yourself. When does your business get done— at social functions or in the office? My advice is not to go to so many social events. The more you are perceived as a successful entrepreneur, the more people will want you to be at every event. The reason is that the more successful people that come to an event, the more successful the event appears to be.

At some point, you have to draw a line. Ask yourself, "Is this a good connection for me?" Pick and choose the events you attend. Otherwise, if you're out every night, you are, first of all, wasting money. Second, you are not going to be effective in the office if you're out every evening late. Third, you could be doing something much more productive with your time in reference to your business unless social events are a part of your business. In the same way that you are investing into your business, I am investing into the people I mentor. It's an investment of my time and energy into someone else's life. I want to have a good return on my investment.

When people talk with me about being mentored, I'm actually interviewing them. I ponder, *Do this person and I see eye to eye?* I'm not trying to change the way you walk your entrepreneurship road, but I do need to see that my time—which is often more valuable to me than my money—is used wisely. By the end of the meeting where you have asked me to mentor you, I'll know "yes" or "no" as to whether or not you are a good investment for me to make with my time and energy. I do have to see eye to eye with you on key issues; we may not be on the same business path, but we have to be going in the same direction.

If your path goes all over the place, around corners, turning back at an angle, then it affects the foundation you are trying to lay. Using the example of the young man who came to see me, if the way that you plan to start your business includes losing two hours a day going to lunch with someone and taking every Friday off when you're not successful, then you and I are not going in the same direction. I can't invest in that. I don't agree with that because I believe you have to put your time in to be successful. If the first thing you do when you start a business is go hire a personal assistant when you really don't have the money, then that's something else I can't agree with. I believe you have to put in the work—pay your dues. If you're willing to do that, I can mentor you. If you just want to have someone sitting in an office while you enjoy your title and all the fun, then we can't work together. That's not how I'm cut out. I can't invest in that.

What I can invest in—what I can give back to—is the entrepreneur who is willing to do the hard work, do the homework, do the 101 basics of business. When I invest in that person, I not only put something into them, I reap rewards for myself and for my company.

Entrepreneur 101 Takeaway:

1. *Mentoring lets you give back—but you can't mentor everyone.*

2. *Look for someone who is willing to do the hard work, who is going the same direction you are going, who has the same general philosophy of how to conduct business.*

3. *Guard your time—it's sometimes worth more than your money—by investing in just a few who show potential for real success.*

CHAPTER 37:

Keep Your How-to's

How-to's are those basic skills we need to run our businesses—but which we forget on a daily basis. How do we communicate? How do we write a contract? How do we create a business plan? How do we orchestrate the next phase of where we are going? My business is medicine; how do I add a new department? The answer to that is I do it the way I added the first department. I take the same procedure that worked for me on the very first time, I make it even better and I have a new department. Someone said to me, "You're a nuclear medicine technologist. How did you know that you could put in a MRI scanner? You're not an MRI tech."

I took my very same concept book on "how to do nuclear medicine" and made it into the "how-to" for MRI, the "how-to" for CT, the "how-to" for real estate. I created my own "how to be a business owner" guidebook. It is the same fundamental, step-by-step guide. The only difference is the particulars; instead of doing MRI, it's carrying out CT or buying real estate. The basic concept doesn't change. This is part of the foundation I created for my business. If you build that "how-to" foundation correctly, it will carry you successfully to every kind of business you want to begin.

You Can Do It Yourself

The "how-to" allows me to transition from one field into new ones. I had never done real estate, but I knew I could do it because I had established my "how-to"—my list of procedures that let you begin a business. I consider it my business plan—not the one I initially wrote to give bankers, but the "real business plan" that I follow today, not five years down the road. My "real business plan" was how to put a nuclear medicine department on wheels. Once I had done that, I had a blueprint for setting up a business. I made a book of the basic documents that I used to start my first company. I kept every single document from when I started the first company and put it into a binder. Why? Because I start a new company every other year or so.

For example, I have every piece of information on how I got my very first federal tax ID number. I sat on the phone with the IRS for close to three hours trying to get that first federal ID number. I learned that I could do that. Today, instead of having my accountant or attorney call when I start a new company, I know I can do it myself. I sit on the phone with the IRS and get the number. My company is started after I get that number.

I learned that the first time you carry out the basic components of starting a business is the hardest; it will never be that hard to begin a new business again. If you document everything you did and save your entry paperwork, you will have your own step-by-step guide for each aspect of that process. You will create the "how- to" of getting the federal ID number, creating your operating agreement, of selecting an accountant. After you do it the first time, you simply capitalize on what you have done by streamlining that process and making it better. The basic process doesn't change—you simply make it more efficient.

Keep Everything from When You Started

Keep your paperwork. Document everything you did—whether you keep it in your mind or write the steps out. This way, you don't have to reinvent the wheel each time you start a new company. If I can start a business I understand, such as Mobile Nuclear Medicine, then starting one with MRI isn't all that difficult. The basic components are going to be the same. If I am going into real estate, it's a different business but certain aspects remain the same. It builds on your confidence. I know that if I can start one business, I can start others. I have my blueprint. The details change from business to business, but there are certain fundamentals that are never going to change. As a new entrepreneur you should be involved in every process at the beginning. You know how it works and when it is time to move onto something new, you can do it.

The first time I started a business, I hired professionals to do most aspects of the work. For example, I paid someone $12,000 to do my operating agreement and get my Oklahoma certificate. The second time, I knew what had to be done. I had been there myself, involved in every step, and I had asked for a copy of the agreement. I don't mean just a paper copy. I asked for an electronic copy of the agreement. We live in the computer age.

Get an Electronic Copy

Every document I have paid to have created I get as either a PDF or as a Word document. Once I have the electronic copy, for example, of the LLC, am I going to pay an attorney to write another? No, I'm not going to do that! I will take the old company name out of the electronic document, add the new company's name and make whatever necessary changes are required in the partnership agreement. How hard is that? It's not hard at all! I can do it and save my time and money in the process.

Because I sat on the phone the first time and obtained my federal ID number, I learned how it was done. Too many entrepreneurs want to sit on the sidelines and hire a professional to do these things. No, you have to know the process for yourself. You don't have to be the expert, but you need to learn the process for yourself. After I paid that first $12,000 for the LLC agreement, I can now set up my own operating agreements for an LLC and for an S-Corp. I took every document, every piece of paper, laminated it and placed it in a binder. I still have my first loan agreement in my "manual" that I created. Every document, every process—I put it in my binder. I still have that information.

Did I really know what I was doing when I started saving those things? No, I didn't. When I started my company, I thought it was my one and only company. But in hindsight, I realize that saving every piece of paper, documenting every process that I did, set me up for a level of success on a path that would allow me to have many companies. I didn't know what I was doing was an excellent idea. I had no mentor, no one telling me to do this. I simply felt I had to know everything involved in starting my company. And it paid off.

The next year, when I went to start my second company, I already had my LLC agreement. I knew that I could call the IRS myself for my federal ID number. I knew that I could register my company with the state and get my name listed. Because I already knew how to do these things, in less than twenty-four hours I had another company. Those were my "how-to's." Don't reinvent the wheel or pay someone else to do it each time you repeat a process. You have to participate in your life, and you have to know what people are doing for you. You don't necessarily have to do it your-self the first time, but you do have to know what is going on. I was like a window shopper, watching someone dress the mannequins. I observed everything going on—the next time, I knew what to do.

I created my own manual on how to start a business. If you are going to go through all of this sweat and strain the first time, some of which is painful, you might as well benefit from it in a real way. Get involved in every process. Observe those professionals you hired the first time. Learn how they did it. Get those electronic copies—even if they don't want to give them to you. Trust me, your accountant, your CPA, everyone will complain about sending them to you, because the moment you have those documents, you're a free person. For example, once I get the electronic copies of my taxes, quarterly statements, etc. I don't have to call any tax accountant for copies of these documents because everything is on my computer.

Don't Pay Someone Else to Reinvent the Wheel

From this point, I'm no longer interested in the paper copies. I'm not going to call you every time I need a new document and have you charge me for it. No, I want the electronic version. I can make the changes. My motto is that if I paid for it, I want a copy. This has been part of the learning experience, part of my journey.

Early on, I had an accounting firm send me an electronic copy of my operating agreement. They didn't want to do that because now I have that component and can create my own whenever I start a new company.

Too many new entrepreneurs think they have to spend a tremendous amount of money on having someone else create their business for them. Instead, go talk to someone who has successfully done it on their own. I have helped ten or fifteen other people start their own businesses. Once you know what you're doing, once you have the electronic documents and you know the steps to each process, starting your business can be a matter of minutes of work.

Once you get your federal ID number, you go to the bank and open an account. Next, you create your operating agreement for your LLC. After that, you call the state to register your company—and you're done. Four basic things, and you are in business and you are legal. An attorney will tell you not to do these things for yourself because they need you to need them. No, you don't need an attorney to set up your company! He's not going to do anything differently except charge you.

I'm not saying you do not need to get legal and professional advice because that is a part of building your professional team. We can't be experts in all areas.

Don't limit this "how-to" process to just setting up a new company. Document everything you do for the first time. Look at the ways you can make it better—more efficient. Streamline the process—and profit from your painful first experiences. I still have my "manual," even though I haven't pulled it out in many years. I kept every loan application. I have my first tax ID form. I have the first operating agreement—every document that allowed me to start that company. I kept these because I was involved with every single aspect. I kept everything because I realized I didn't even know what I didn't know! Instead, I kept everything, put it in the book and organized it according to what it was. I have the first loan on that $654,000 truck, my first tax permit from 1998, the city code with my number on it and a copy of the first investment check someone gave me. I kept copies of everything. I have a copy of where an attorney filed for me with the Oklahoma Secretary of State—and charged me $500 for it. This is something that you can do online, and it only costs approximately $100.

So many people don't realize that they can do much of their work for themselves. I am not suggesting that you don't need someone to help with your legal work, but the moment that you have it done and get those files, you can expand outside that box of being dependent on someone else. This is part of developing your confidence as an entrepreneur. You know that you can do it for yourself—you don't need to pay other people to do it for you. It's part of the journey—and it's part of learning to soar.

Entrepreneurial 101 Takeaway:

1. *Keep the five, ten or twenty documents that you first used to start your business.*

2. *Keep them in sequential order, and document when they were done—and why.*

3. *This is your blueprint—this is your business "how-to."*

CHAPTER 38:

You Can!

Every entrepreneur needs to have this mind-set: Failure is not an option! If you can keep this attitude, it takes away all of the negativity, all of the fear. It removes the stereotypes of that glass ceiling. If you believe that you can make this business happen, then no matter how hard it is, no matter how many days you are challenged, no matter how tough the road gets or how dark the clouds are, you will know that tomorrow is going to be a different day.

For the real entrepreneur, tomorrow is always a different day. The pressures you face today are not the ones that you will confront tomorrow. As long as you know that you can do this, you can have that positive energy. I like to tell entrepreneurs, "You just have to keep pushing forward."

The Journey Can Be Rough—Get Ready

Part of what helped me believe "I can" was that I didn't have an option for failure. My son was six months old—what else could I do? I had to keep thinking, *I can.* Every day I had to know that I could. I can. I am. Every day the sun would come up and go back down, and each day was a different day. I found that the road was always going to have rough spots. There is no road for an entrepreneur that is always just peachy. I don't know anyone—and I know a number of entrepreneurs—for whom life is always incredible. It just doesn't happen like that. This entrepreneur journey is an incredible process of learning what you need to know and how you are supposed to operate. So decide today: "I can." It's a simple concept—and don't allow yourself to think otherwise. Giving yourself no option to fail, deciding that you can, is absolutely vital to your success.

For women especially, this is a real change in mentality. We are often told that we can do certain things—we can manage a house and raise our children—but maybe we can't run a business. I was told that many times just driving the truck. It was a man's environment. After all, how many women truck drivers were there? Now there are quite a few, but when I started my business, there weren't many. People didn't have a great deal of faith in a woman driving a truck around rural Oklahoma to deliver nuclear medicine diagnostic services. Because of that, many people weren't interested in investing in my company. This turned out to be a blessing in disguise—I didn't have a large group to buy out later. However, I had to face those negative opinions. Even though many people didn't think I could make a success of this business, I believed I could. I did make a success of it, and now I know that "I can."

You Start with What You Know

"I can" mentality is the one every entrepreneur must have. You need to know that you can do it no matter how hard it is—and it is going to be hard. There are going to be some incredibly hard times.

You need to know that "you can." The true entrepreneur ideas don't just come out of thin air. They originate with you knowing that you have a skill, the basic knowledge. Most entrepreneurs have been breeding those ideas in their minds for months if not years. Most entrepreneurs do not wake up tomorrow and say, "You know what? I'm going to start a restaurant. I don't have the first idea how to do it, I don't know anything at all about the food industry, but I just think I'll do this."

The idea that lets you say "I can" is the one that has been brewing and churning inside you, developing a life on its own until it begins to overpower the negative thoughts of failure. That idea begins to overpower you. That's when you have to talk about it and tell the world, "Hey, I am going to start an imaging center!" People may come back and say, "Oh, no, you can't! That's not possible." But you know that you can. You know that you have the industry experience, drive, power, energy and knowledge.

Where Does the Dream Begin?

These dreams rise organically from the base of knowledge and skill that you have. Being able to start my first business came from the knowledge and the skills I had as a technologist. Once I had started that business, I had that base within me to know that if I could start one business, I could start another. With the true entrepreneur, ideas begin to arise and start boiling within you. The ideas get bigger until they overwhelm you—but they start with a base in your real knowledge and ability.

People do come up with ideas such as going out and buying a franchise when they don't have a clue as to how to run it. That's not how the entrepreneur works. When it comes to someone investing in your idea, you have to be able to demonstrate that you have some credibility in terms of knowing that field and how it operates. You have to have some basis in reality for that idea. Your venture is going to require capital. It will require time, energy and a location. The entrepreneur is the one with the idea that he or she *knows* what can be done because of their background in that area. Why did I think that I could start a mobile nuclear medicine service? I knew I could because I was a nuclear medicine tech. I knew the field. I had the skills. And because of that, I was passionate about my dream and I knew "I can!"

Entrepreneur 101 Takeaway:

1. *The real entrepreneur ideas come from what is already in you—you are your knowledge and skills combined with your passion.*

2. *Allow those ideas to grow until they become bigger than all of the negativity you will get from others without your vision.*

3. *Then develop that "I can" mentality—don't let failure be an option!*

CHAPTER 39:

Feel Your Confidence

We have already touched on this topic of confidence, but I want to approach it from a different angle. When you start the entrepreneur journey, you don't have the confidence you need. It is an aspect of this path that has to be developed. I think of it as a baby starting to walk and talk. A newborn infant can't do either—those skills come with time and maturity. It's the same way with confidence. We may start with a little of it. We have the basics. We have certain skills and abilities. Then, we begin to venture out. We use that "I can" attitude. We focus our attention on the task at hand—and we succeed because we earned that success with our hard work. Confidence begins to grow. Confidence breeds more confidence with each success.

Confidence Is Developed

Confidence grows on the entrepreneur journey. Today I know that I exude confidence—I walk around with it. However, when I started out running this company, I didn't have as much confidence as I do today. Every day in a new business, you deal with hoping you and your business survive. Your confidence sits there quivering and shaking for the most part until you begin to have those moments of success that build for you. Those successes, one on top of the other, allow you to have and exude confidence. That's when you find that positive level where things begin to go your way. Confidence comes from success. It develops. New entrepreneurs need to know that they won't start with all the confidence they need. But as you move from one success to another—success you have earned with hard work and keeping your eyes on the path, with living in the now—you will develop confidence.

I will say this again, *failure cannot be an option for you*. When I started this company with a huge truck payment and a son who was six months old, it was the same situation I faced when I graduated from high school. I didn't take the vocational education classes. I didn't know how to type. I had backed myself into a corner because I didn't have anything to fall back on. I literally had no skill set to fall back on. I was a female. How was I going to take care of myself? I didn't have the option to go to work at Hertz. I purposely put myself in the situation where I had only one option. I had to go to college and get a skill, find a career.

Monthly Payments on a $654,000 Truck

When I started my business, I didn't have a choice. I had a son and a truck payment. I had to succeed. I had been making $50,000 a year, and now I had to make a $10,000 a month truck payment. Once again, I didn't have an option. It was either make that payment or ruin my credit for the next ten years. I backed myself into my own personal corners. I had to be successful because I could only go in one direction. I could never use reverse, because I didn't put a reverse in the plan!

I also didn't create the possibility of failure by the putting pressure on myself in looking so far down the road that I could never enjoy the small successes. I didn't give myself the option of stacking one failure on top of the other. No, I positioned myself for one small success after the other. Those successes began to stack up. They created the confidence that grew within me, and that confidence created an environment for further successes. The two function as a cycle.

I tell every starting entrepreneur: Create small successes. Let those successes build your confidence. Feel that confidence grow in you on the entrepreneur journey—your confidence allows you to take each successive step on the entrepreneurial journey with boldness!

Entrepreneurial 101 Takeaway:

1. *Don't let failure be an option—if necessary, back yourself into the corner that will spur you on to the hard work you need.*

2. *Know that the tiny successes lead to bigger ones. Let them accumulate.*

3. *Your success breeds confidence—let confidence grow until you are up to the challenges that a successful business will bring your way!*

CHAPTER 40:

The Balancing Act

A question I am asked constantly is, "How do you balance your personal life with your life as a businesswoman?" People wonder if I ever go home, if I ever sleep. Of course I sleep, and of course I go home. I do, however, look back to the beginning days with this company, being a single parent, not having enough support for my son, listening to people tell me I was a bad mother, my son constantly saying, "Mommy, no" every time we went to the office. It was a journey.

I was fortunate to have a wonderful family living next door to me—the Reeds. They recognized that I had a crazy schedule with this new venture. They would pick up my six-month- old son, and they would take care of him. It wasn't without difficulty! They are an Anglo-American family, and once while I was on the road, they had him for longer than usual. They washed his hair and panicked when it didn't "go back" to the way it had been before. They thought they had ruined his hair. They were incredibly kind to both of us. My son and I are still very close to them. Having them in our lives gave me the support I needed for him at that crucial time.

The Early Days Can Be Tough

Eventually, I learned not to work until 11:00 or 12:00 P.M. every night and not to work every Saturday and Sunday. Slowly, I achieved balance. At first, I did have to work, and I make no apologies for the life my son and I led. Many times, women entrepreneurs and business owners get made out to be bad parents because we have to commit to our work sometimes at the cost of being with our children as much as we wish. We don't have a wife at home taking care of the business of a family. Those early years were just plain tough. However, as more business success started to come and life was easier, we started to hire more people. I was able to balance and I married a great guy. He and my son bonded. There was a new stability in our lives, a new balance for us. Now, my son is at the office almost every day, and as I have said, he has his own office where he can study or play or watch TV. He has his own workout room. I have been able to create balance for him and for me and my husband.

I once had a doctor ask me, "How do you stay married? How do you balance?" I didn't even know he knew I was married, but obviously he had done his research before he came to our meeting. As I have said, it's fortunate that my husband works with us. He has a significant role in the company, and he manages all of the real estate companies. This gives me the flexibility to achieve what I want because he carries a significant part of the load. We can buy as much real estate as I want, but can I go out and check on it all? No. Can I answer all the calls? No. I am able to do those things because of my husband being the support and the backbone I need for what I do.

People often say that behind every great man is a great woman, but in this situation, behind every great woman there has to be a great man facilitating all of this. Before I was married to my husband, it was always a struggle trying to get people to help me.

We had to *learn* to work together. When we first got married, he wasn't the guy who stayed at work until 8:00 or 9:00 at night. He worked for a major corporation and observed "regular" hours. It's not that he had to become a workaholic, but he did have to learn how I worked. Now, if I am at work until 7:00 or 8:00, my husband is with me, and the three of us go home together every night. We have had our disagreements—and all relationships, business or personal, have disagreements—but we learned to understand our separate roles. Early on, we did a balancing act in that area, too. Learning to do that was part of the journey.

Frankly, I could write a whole book on learning to balance business and family when you are a woman business owner. Today, my husband, son and I have a wonderful life—and it has come from achieving balance.

That Work Will Be There Tomorrow

One area of achieving balance is realizing—especially for the "workaholic" type like me who loves this company and has passion for her business—that I could work literally 24/7, 365 days a year if I didn't watch it. I had to realize that I could go home, and I would still have the job to come to the next day. It doesn't matter how long you work at night, you will still have work to do the next day. I have had to learn what is important to do each day—I've had to find my priorities. At first, I attempted to do my entire job every day. You can't do that. Even if you own the business, it's like working for someone else in that the job exists every single day.

Every day there will still be papers on my desk. Tomorrow, no matter how much work I do today, there will still be a pile of work to do—and you want that! It's your job security. Instead of trying to do everything today, you have to balance the work and your personal life. Each day, pick the most pressing and important project for that day. When you finish the last part—writing that invoice, that check, the last protocol or policy—shut down, close the door and go home.

You have to live in the now. You cannot get everything done in one day. That's not possible. The work will be there tomorrow. The smart businesswoman realizes this and works with it. This knowledge helps her work toward balance. I learned to set an internal list of what had to happen that day. Each day, I worked toward accomplishing those goals. Over the years, I have shortened those eighteen-hour days to twelve hours, then to eight or ten. I have to admit that I never work less than eight hours, but I know you can get yourself to the point of a "normal" workday. It just takes time.

Finally, I'm at a place in the business where I can take off Fridays if I want to. I couldn't do that at first, but I can now. One way to achieve balance is to remember that the work will be there tomorrow—and savor that fact. That's the great satisfaction of coming into my office every day. What you have to learn is that once you have finished that last invoice or read that last e-mail, it's time to close up and go home. You're done for the day.

Just for the Women

I do want to address some concerns specifically for women, both single and married. If you are single and you have children, find some method of support that will not only provide for your child's needs when you are at work, but will also give you the break you need on occasion and allow you to have downtime for yourself. When I started my business, I was fortunate to not only have the Reeds but to find some excellent drop-in play centers for my son. I didn't have to call and make an appointment for him or beg them to take him. I didn't have to be back at a set time. They kept him for an hourly rate. I knew he was being taken care of, that he was busy and happy. This allowed me to come into work or run errands or just have a little personal time without interfering so much with his life.

Find at least one, if not more, ways to help yourself. As women, we do so much for other people. On Saturday, I used to get up early to clean the house—and then find myself cleaning all day long. I decided not to do that any longer. Instead, I hired a housekeeper. That way, I didn't have that pressure on Saturday of looking at a house that needed all of my attention—it was still clean! I also had a friend who would help me with the shopping, who would run errands for me. Just those few things allowed me to have some independence, care for my child, keep my life in order and do my work.

Married women deal with the same issues, but often, they have that internal support for the children in their husbands. Still, they have to make a point of taking some quality time for themselves. Even with that support, you have to take time for "self-maintenance." I started making a weekly appointment for self-maintenance. I made a commitment to do just that one thing each week—whether it was my hair or a pedicure or a manicure. I made sure I was doing something just for me each week to keep myself looking and feeling my best. Married women need to keep that in mind. We do so much for our business, for our staff and then we go home and do for our families. That's great—but we need to take care of ourselves. Doing that helps bring the balance we need.

Use a support system! People get used to relying on women to do everything for the family: the grocery shopping, the clothes shopping, cooking, helping with homework, decorating and maintaining the house. All of these still need to happen, but if you have your internal support system, use it. Have some shutdown time just for yourself. One thing that worked for me was to get up at about 5:30 or 6:00 A.M. and enjoy the quiet time which I consider my quality time for me— and that has become my personal quality time every day.

Finally, learn to ask for help. That doesn't always come easy when you are used to running the show at work and being in charge. You will find that when people recognize that you're burning the candle at both ends, they will step up and want to help. Let them in. You're great at helping others—at work and at home. Now, let others help you. That's one more step in the journey of developing the balance you need.

Entrepreneur 101 Takeaway:

1. *Find an external support system if you are single.*

2. *If you're married, enlist your family as your internal support system—they see what you're doing. They want to help!*

3. *Remember to find ways to do something for your self-maintenance and to have quality time alone.*

4. *Balance is a journey—you won't get there in one day. It is developed—and it will allow you to do the work for which you have passion and to have a personal life you love.*

CHAPTER 41:

I'm Done!

There is a time for the entrepreneur to say, "I'm done." That isn't quitting, but rather it's coming to a stage of success where you can say, "Maybe I have done all I can in this arena or on this contract. Maybe I have done everything I can do for you." It's tied to having an exit strategy when you develop your business. How do I decide when it's time to go? How do I go? Am I able to go? Am I still having fun with this business, or is it more stressful than pleasurable?

Where Is the Excitement?

I think that in order for an entrepreneur to have true success, there needs to be some moments of joy, some "shooting stars," some exclamation points in the middle of the striving and the stress. Once those are gone, it's time to say, "I'm done." And in saying that, you need an exit strategy. What's next? I know for myself—and I think I speak for the majority of true entrepreneurs—I can't just sit and do nothing. I have been so busy, so used to being active and making decisions, being an actor and not a spectator in my business, that I don't think I can be idle. I don't think I can just "shut down."

Saying, "I'm done" comes in many forms. You have to be able to listen to the inner you to figure out when that time comes for you. And you have to develop an exit strategy. Honestly, my exit strategy is still a work in progress, even after ten years into having this company. Developing that strategy is part of the journey I'm on as an entrepreneur. I do know that our lives tell us when it's time to move on. When you find little reward in your accomplishments no matter how great they are, then it's time to move on. When the work just becomes "business as usual" and there is no passion and fulfillment in climbing that mountain—or when you see no more mountains to climb—then it's time to say, "I'm done."

The truth is that if you grow your company properly, it will eventually become "just business" and day-to-day operations. When it does that, do you leave or stay? That's a hard question for most entrepreneurs because they gave birth to this "baby" and raised it. When it "grows up," it's hard to let go of it. However, if you have "raised it right," someone else will want it. It's just like your child growing up and getting married. If you raise him right, someone else is going to want to take over from there!

When Do You Say, "I'm Done"?

You need to be able to recognize when that time comes. You have to be adult enough to let it go. Sometimes your company can outgrow you to where it is too large for you to manage with the management style that you have and that is authentic to you. It all comes back to having that new mountain to climb, that new challenge, the new "something" to do. There comes a point where your new mountain isn't in your company anymore. You can't run it the way it needs to be run.

As your business grows and develops, you have to reassess how to manage it. A few years ago, I had a manager who told me his company was two miles down the road and there was no way of catching it. He said that the company was growing at such a rate that it was becoming difficult to manage within current guidelines. I agree that my company is growing. I want my company to grow—but I also want to be able to manage the growth. Sometimes you have to face the fact that your company can now use a bigger management system. Sometimes the best thing for the company is for you to walk away from it—best for the company itself, best for the staff, best for the clients and best for you.

The Journey Never Ends

That's not the end. There are more mountains to climb, more goals to achieve, more problems to conquer. The true entrepreneur carries that spirit of adventure within, knowing that the "I'm done" of today in one area leads to the excitement of the next venture—business or personal—just around the corner, down the path on the road. Keep that excitement alive. Keep that passion burning "I'm done" is the beginning of the next chapter in your journey.

Entrepreneur Takeaway 101:

1. *Plan your exit—even if it's a work in progress.*

2. *Look for the signs it's time to go—your passion is gone, there are no more challenges, your business needs a new management style.*

3. *When you leave, remember: "I'm done" can be the door into the next challenge. The true entrepreneur continues to walk the road and experience the journey!*